WITHDRAWN
HARVARD LIBRARY
WITHDRAWN

Morals Based on Needs

Ragnar Ohlsson

University Press of America Inc.
Lanham • New York • London

Copyright © 1995 by
University Press of America,® Inc.
4720 Boston Way
Lanham, Maryland 20706

3 Henrietta Street
London, WC2E 8LU England

All rights reserved
Printed in the United States of America
British Cataloging in Publication Information Available

Library of Congress Cataloging-in-Publication Data

Ohlsson, Ragnar.
Morals based on needs / Ragnar Ohlsson.
p. cm.
Includes bibliographical references and index.
1. Ethics. 2. Need (Philosophy) I. Title.
BJ1470.2.O35 1995
171'.7—dc20   94-46307 CIP

ISBN 0-8191-9853-6 (cloth: alk paper)

㊀™ The paper used in this publication meets the minimum
requirements of American National Standard for Information Sciences—Permanence of Paper for
Printed Library Materials,
ANSI Z39.48-1984

Contents

Acknowledgements ix

Introduction xi

Chapter 1 Interests 1

Living beings have two kinds of interests:
a) they have goals which they desire to attain on their own account;
b) certain conditions are necessary if they are to attain any of their goals, i.e. they have *needs*. 1
I cannot but want other persons to treat me as I want to be treated; therefore no principle exhorting us to do something towards others not wanted by these persons can be consistently upheld. 3
Needs, however, are more important from the moral point of view, since, whatever you want, your needs must be satisfied. 7
Moral statements can be interpreted as claims which it is reasonable to put forward by individuals with needs and desires. 13

Chapter 2 A Central Concept in Western Philosophy 19

In ancient Greek moral philosophy we meet with the first attempts to distinguish between 'necessary' and 'unnecessary desires'. 19
In the early Christian community needs are for the first time taken to be relevant to the question of what constitutes a just distribution. 21
Hegel and Marx base much of their theories on the concept of 'need' and discuss the relativity of needs. 22
During the early decades of this century a lot of psychological research is devoted to finding out which the fundamental human drives and needs are. 26

Some philosophers make use of a distinction between "true" and "false needs". 26
In our time the needs are related to the question of the earth's limited resources. 27
The last section is a discussion of the question whether there are some interesting and common notions in these discussions. It is pointed out that the distinctions and concepts are connected with the Greek philosophical project of basing an objectively valid ethical system on human nature. 28
Lastly the question of the relativity of needs is discussed. This problem is today graver than it used to be, since we see the possibilities of changing nature by genetic manipulation. It is argued that at least some questions concerning the desirability and undesirability of certain changes of needs nonetheless can be answered within the framework of a moral system of the type proposed. 33

Chapter 3 **The Modern Discussion of Needs** 37

I. Needs as innate desires.
Herbert Marcuse call innate desires "true needs". 38
Abraham Maslow constructed his famous hierarchy of needs from studies of "healthy individuals". It is argued that there is a circularity built into this way of delimiting the class of needs. Furthermore it seems to involve normative decisions. 40

II. Needs as necessary conditions. 43
Many authors have analysed 'needs' as "necessary conditions for avoiding harm". None of them however analyses 'harm' in a satisfactory way. 43
David Braybrooke connects needs with "a normal human life", 45
David Miller with a "plan of life", 45
Georg Henrik von Wright with "human welfare", 46
Garrett Thomson analyses "needs" in terms of "avoiding harm". What constitutes harm is determined by our interests, which are not what we usually understand by this term, but rather some form of innate, unconscious elements of our motivational set up. However, Thomson does not draw the line between harm and non-harm in a very definite way. 48
Many authors want more requirements fulfilled to call something a need, since they think that a need-statement gives rise to a legitimate claim. Further conditions on 'need' such as compatibility

and moral restrictions are rejected. 51

III. Needs and justice. 54
The concept of 'need' is often found in discussions of justice.
David Miller takes the principle "to each according to his needs" to
be one of three main candidates for a substantial principle of justice.
But Miller's own interpretation of this principle seems to be
unsatisfactory. 54
Some other interpretations of the socialist slogan "to each according
to his needs" are discussed, but all of them are found defective in
some way. 58
The conclusion is that intuitions concerning justice are too
vague. Rawls, Rescher, and Sterba all try to safeguard a minimal
level of well-being. They are on the right track, but the principle
"to each according to his needs" gives a more reasonable principle
if interpreted as a principle of rights as proposed in Ch. 6. 61

IV. 'Need' as a bridge between 'is' and 'ought'. 64
'Need' seems to be both an empirical and a normative concept.
Several authors with leanings towards naturalism have analysed
the connection between 'need' and 'ought' 64

Chapter 4 **Desires** 69

By "desire" I refer to all kinds of positive and negative attitudes
taken to be behavioural dispositions. 70
Some problems of such an analysis are discussed. 71
In this wide class of behavioural dispositions I distinguish between
a) intrinsic and instrumental desires; 74
b) self-related desires and those concerning others; 76
c) those actual desires that would change if the bearer of the
attitudes were fully informed and those that would not. Only the
latter are accorded moral relevance. 78
Some other conditions are formulated: the attitudes are not the
result of involuntary hypnosis, 81
nor influenced by drugs, 82
nor the result of brainwashing or other kinds of
illegitimate manipulation. 83
But attitudes that are the result of genetic manipulation are
to be regarded as morally relevant. 83
When it comes to animals and persons with grave brain damage
and the like, their desires are morally relevant, but the conditions

of stability in spite of new information, etc, are replaced by
considerations of benevolent keepers. 85
These attitudes are morally relevant, because:
a) the attitudes in this class are the ones we want satisfied;
b) to take them seriously is to respect individuals' autonomy
c) what is characteristic of these attitudes is that they are difficult
to change (in a morally acceptable way), therefore you cannot ask
if it would be better to change the attitudes rather than satisfy them. 85
Three problems with this account are discussed:
a) How are we to measure the quantity of desire satisfaction? The
answer is that we let the persons involved choose between rather
big parts of lives. 86
b) Can actual desire-satisfaction unknown to the person concerned
make her life better? And how are we to explain that Othello,
although satisfied, is suffering? In some cases at least we rather
want our desires to be satisfied than know that this is
the case. 88
c) If you could relieve a neurotic person of his compulsive
behaviour by secretly giving him a drug that he does not want
to take, would this not be right, if the person after taking
the drug, accepted it? With some hesitation I answer no. 89
d) The question whether we ought to exclude morally blameworthy
desires (such as sadistic desires) is discussed and given a negative
answer: they are to be included in the moral calculation, given that
they fulfil the other conditions, but the value of their satisfaction
must be weighed against the negative effects on the desire-
satisfaction of other beings. 90

Chapter 5 **Needs** 93

"Needs" are defined as "necessary and in the situation sufficient
conditions for some goal". 95
Although several different kinds of entities can be said to need this
or that, the normatively interesting needs belong to living
organisms. 95
What is needed is some state. 96
Need-statements with no mention of goal are elliptical. 96
Needs are not only acute lacks or wants. 98
Needs are in some ways relative to circumstances, 98
but the basic needs do not change from society to society or during
history. 100
Basic needs must be satisfied, 101

or else someone will suffer harm. 102
We need what is necessary to survive if we have prospects of
living at least a minimally acceptable life, i.e. a life which
is better than being dead. 103
If we cannot possibly live a minimally acceptable life, we need
the means to be painlessly unconscious. 104
Whether a life of some individual is worth living or not, is up to
her to decide. 104
Some needs are necessary to avoid grave illness and/or handicap;
such needs must be satisfied if we are to have acceptable although
not minimally acceptable lives. Some such need can be
frustrated without life being so bad that death is preferable. Thus
there is a certain - but vague - distance between the two
levels 'acceptable' and 'minimally acceptable life'. 106
Lastly it is argued that there are some necessary conditions for
living a human life: freedom and education. It is argued that
they are needed to a degree that is to be determined in relation to
each society by rational and well-informed persons by
unanimous consensus. 109
The analysis is summarized:
The individual B has a basic need for C-ing x in the situation s,
if and only if C-ing x is necessary and sufficient for B in s to
live an acceptable life, or – if there is no chance of
attaining a minimally acceptable life – C-ing x is necessary
and sufficient in s to bring B's suffering to an end. 111

Chapter 6 **Rights** 115

Every human being has a right to need-satisfaction,
and a right to strive for satisfaction of her desires, as long as this
does not conflict with the equal or stronger rights of other beings. 115
This principle is to be interpreted in the following way:
a) A right is a morally or legally guaranteed status; in this context
a valid system of *moral* rights is sought. 116
b) The right to need-satisfaction is both negative and positive, i.e.
no one should prevent anyone from obtaining need-satisfaction and
everyone has an obligation to help others satisfy them if necessary. 116
c) The right to strive for desire satisfaction is mainly negative,
except for those tied together by personal relations. 116
d) A moral right is justified by the importance of the things
guaranteed to the individual. We should therefore try to reduce

violations of rights to as few as possible. 117
The proposed principle couldbe validated according to an idea
proposed by T.M. Scanlon: it should be possible to justify a
moral norm to others. 120
Some intutive moral arguments in favour of the principles are
given:
a) What is important from this point of view is what happens to
individuals. 126
b) To everyone need-satisfaction is more important than the
satisfaction of desires. 126
c) The principles express an idea of respect for persons as
autonomous agents. 127
d) What is felt as unacceptably unjust is not so much
unequal distribution of satisfaction but that a moral principle
without constraints on the worst outcomes can imply that you
ought to let some people suffer severely to make life better for
the rest. 127
Objections to the principles are discussed: 127
a) The difference between individuals is not morally important;
this is rejected. 127
b) A correct moral principle is not person-affecting in a strong
sense; this is rejected. 130
c) It is pointless to save people if we have to sacrifice all
satisfaction of desire; the principle is modified to meet the
objection. 132
d) It is no point in guaranteeing rights if this does not lead to
positive consequences; it is shown that this is not a consequence
of the proposed theory. 135
e) The theory provides no obvious solution to the problem of
our moral obligations towards animals, and how these obligations
are to be weighed against obligations towards human beings.
The conclusion is that the greatest problem is the delimitation
of the class of right holders. The theory can, however be
modified to justify our obligations towards animals. 137

Bibliography 143

Index 149

Acknowledgements

Some persons have read earlier versions of this manusript. None of them has shared all my convictions or accepted all my arguments. This has forced me to modify my standpoints in some ways and to try to sharpen the arguments but in no substantial way changed my views. Kai Sørlander has a deep interest in the concept of 'need' and its implications for ethics. I have profited a lot from his long letters and detailed criticisms of my manusript. Lars Bergström, Torbjörn Tännsjö and Jan Österberg have read the entire manuscript and made many valuable suggestions of improvements. Christoph Fehige read some parts of the manuscript and made good points, some of which have influenced the final version. Many other friends and colleagues at the Department of Philosophy of Stockholm University have discussed various points in the essay. David Jones has tried to rid my text of the most blatant mistakes in the English language. I owe all these persons a deeply felt thank. Swedish Council for Research in Humanities and Social Sciences has given financial support for the publication costs.

Introduction

Like many other philosophers I take as the basis for morality the fact that we have interests and that our good is to satisfy these interests. But my conclusion is that needs are far more important from the moral point of view than other interests such as desires, wants, likes and dislikes. We all want this or that, we like some things and dislike others, desire to obtain some states and shun others. When we get what we want, we are satisfied, and this is what makes our lives worthwhile to ourselves.

Although this is true, the fundamental moral requirement is that we contribute to the satisfaction of needs. Every living being has interests of two kinds: one is that our desires should be satisfied – at least those desires which would not change in the light of new and true information (including experience), and we have an even more basic interest, which is that the necessary conditions for any desire-satisfaction obtain. We need these conditions to obtain. It is from this source that the moral import of needs stems.

In the first chapter the central theses and the main structure of the argument are presented. Human beings have interests, which they try to safeguard by the moral norms they try to get accepted by mutual agreement. These interests are to get their desires satisfied and to guarantee the necessary conditions for their satisfaction. As a general rule the guarantees for the necessary conditions of an acceptable life are much more important to each individual, and therefore for the community, than are the efforts to maximize satisfaction.

The second chapter traces the connections between my standpoint and some of the central themes of European moral philosophy: the ancient distinction between 'necessary' and 'non-necessary desires' is interpreted as related to the distinction between 'needs' and 'desires'. The third chapter is a discussion of the role played by needs in a reasonable normative system according to some 20th century thinkers. The fourth chapter is devoted to an analysis of the concept of 'desire'. It is argued

Morals Based on Needs

that satisfaction of those desires which will not change under the influence of new true information (and which meet certain other conditions) is what makes a life good. Nonetheless the connection between desire-satisfaction and norms is weak: we are not morally required to maximize desire-satisfaction. The fifth chapter analyses 'needs' as necessary and in the situation sufficient conditions for an acceptable life, the latter taken to be a basis for acting freely and striving to reach one's goals. The last chapter sketches a theory of rights, ascribing to human beings a negative and positive right to need-satisfaction, and a negative right to strive for satisfaction of desires. It is argued that such a system expresses the fundamental importance of the necessary conditions for a worthwhile life, the respect we ought to show other human beings as autonomous agents, that these rights are in accordance with our moral intuitions, and that the requirements express claims we all have good reasons to try to get respected by mutual agreement. Thus the system tries to formulate a naturalistic theory both of the genesis and of the validation of morality. Lastly it is discussed whether such a moral system can be widened to include also our obligations towards animals.

Chapter 1

Interests

Human beings and other animals have interests: they want this and that, they like some things and shun others, and they have needs that must be satisfied. The main idea to be formulated and defended in this essay is that living beings have two kinds of interests: they have goals they strive for and there are necessary conditions for their attaining these goals. (Cf Bergström 1970.) The latter kind of interests is the more important one from the view-point of each individual, simply because these must be satisfied if any goals are to be realized. I will further argue that we ought to respect individuals, and that this implies that we cannot trade off the frustration of vital needs for some individual – which means that he suffers or dies – against a greater sum of desire-satisfaction for a lot of people. In fact I will take one step more and argue that, as a general rule, desire-satisfaction is not a moral imperative at all. What is morally important is that we safe-guard the need-satisfaction of each individual, and respect her right to strive for satisfaction of her desires.

What is desired is valuable

Today there is a wide – although not complete – consensus on the idea that what is valuable is to get one's desires satisfied. An early representative of this idea is William James:

> Take any demand, however slight, which any creature, however weak, may make. Ought it not, for its own sole sake, to be satisfied? If not, prove why not. (James 1897, quotation from the 1905 edition, 195)

William James' thesis is that a demand gives rise to a presumption that someone ought to get what she demands. If you do not agree, you must give an argument. The burden of proof rests with him who denies that the demand ought to be satisfied.[1] The position of William James can seem reasonable; I myself find it the most plausible idea put forward concerning what has intrinsic value. But I believe that in the end it is not fully acceptable. Nothing has intrinsic value in the traditional sense of "intrinsic value". And we have no obligation to satisfy desires. But to reach that conclusion I will reason step by step away from James' initially plausible standpoint.

What can be desired are states: you want that this or that should be the case. If a desired state is the case, your desire is satisfied, whether or not you know it. To say that desire-satisfaction is valuable and that it is valuable that a desired state is realized is to say the same thing.[2] Of course "desire-satisfaction" can also refer to felt satisfaction, i. e. the pleasurable consciousness of satisfaction. But I use "satisfaction" to refer to the fact that what is desired is brought about, since this seems to me to be the most reasonable standpoint.

One argument that this is so is the following. Let us assume that some kind of states are valuable, say that someone experiences pleasure. Why are these states valuable? A hedonist in the narrow sense either says that pleasure is good as a matter of contingent fact; the best you can do is to give inductive evidence to this effect: this state of pleasure is good, and so is that, and so forth. Or he maintains that "pleasure is good" is a conceptual truth. Neither answer seems convincing.

Few are hedonists in this narrow sense – as a matter of fact Torbjörn

---

[1] I take it that by "demand" James means every kind of desire; in later parts of the same text James uses "desire" interchangeably with demand See e.g. a few lines further on:"The only possible reason there can be why any phenomenon ought to exist is that such a phenomenon actually is desired." It is true that a possible interpretation of James would be that he maintains an epistemic idea: that to be desired indicates that something has intrinsic value, but not that being desired and having intrinsic value is one and the same. But in other places in the same text it becomes clear that James not only adheres to the epistemological view but also the ontological. See for instance the same essay, 197: "...the metaphysical question in ethical question is sufficiently answered, and /.../ we have learned what the words 'good', 'bad', and 'obligation' severally mean."

[2] Cf Ralph Barton Perry: "Any object, whatever it be, acquires value when any interest, whatever it be, is taken in it." (Perry 1926, 115f.)

Tännsjö is the only one I know of: he takes the first line of argument (Tännsjö 1990 I). Most classical hedonists, like Bentham and Mill, argue that pleasure is good, because it is desired. And then it seems as if their ultimate standpoint as regards intrinsic value is not that pleasure is good, but that desire-satisfaction is what counts. At least desires are morally relevant, although it might be only one necessary condition of intrinsic value: to be intrinsically valuable something has to have at least two characteristics: it is desired or liked for its own sake, and it is experienced. If not experienced, it cannot make a human life either better or worse, so they argue. Thus only desired experiences can be intrinsically good, and such experiences that are desired for their own sake are called "pleasures".[3] Bentham takes it to be a psychological fact that no other experiences (and nothing else either) are desired except pleasures.[4] This seems to be false: we do intrinsically desire other things besides experiences. Therefore the restriction that only experiences can have intrinsic value seems gratuitous.

A further – and to me even more convincing – argument to the effect that what is intrinsically desired is intrinsically valuable is the following. It seems as if you have reached the ultimate basis of reason, when you can state that you want something realized for its own sole sake. If you know what someone wants in and for itself, and know what she believes about the means to realize her desires, you know what can be known about what would motivate her actions. I cannot but let my actions be influenced by my attitudes, choices, and desires. I cannot choose to do what I do not want. When I have conflicting desires I must of course act against some of my desires – but my voluntary actions simply express my choices.[5] Of course in many situations we are

---

[3] John Stuart Mill: "...desiring a thing, and finding it pleasant, /are/ in the strictness of language, two modes of naming the same psychological fact." (Mill 1964, 36) Henry Sidgwick: "I propose /.../ to define Pleasure as a feeling which /.../ is at least impicitly apprehended as desirable .... " (Sidgwick 1966, 127) Sidgwick has already defined "desirable" as "what would be desired, with strength proportional to the degree of desirability, if it were judged attainable by voluntary action, supposing the desirer to possess a perfect forecast, emotional as well as intellectual of the state of attainment or fruition." (Sidgwick 1966, 111)

[4] Jeremy Bentham: " Nothing can act of itself as a motive but the ideas of pleasure and pain." (Bentham 1879, 101f)

[5] According to many philosophers (e.g. Donald Davidson) this is true by definition. Thus the proposition that I cannot choose an action against my will is trivial. The truism is consistent with the assumptions that I can want to do good to others, that I can desire x because I

forced to choose among things none of which we want; but of these bad things we choose the one we consider the best, i. e. we choose the one we want most in the sense that we want this thing rather than the other. If I choose my own actions, I choose the one that will bring about what I most want. I could not at the same time want other persons to treat me in a way I would not choose myself. It would be inconsistent to want to be treated differently from the way one wants to be treated.[6] If you choose to bring about those states that have intrinsic value for other people, in the case they dislike what objectively has intrinsic value, while you choose for yourself only what you want, you treat other people in a way you do not treat yourself. You make an exception for yourself. "Treat others as they want to be treated," can be universally accepted, while the norm "see to it that people get as great a surplus of intrinsically valuable experiences as possible, whether they want them or not," is not. You cannot give this latter norm your full support in all situations: you cannot want others to do that to you, if you abhor these experiences. There is an inconsistency in attitudes – not a logical one – in the latter norm, which is not the case with the first one. Therefore the first one is better.

Assume that a person intrinsically desires among other things that certain states obtain just because he believes that they have intrinsic value. Now he believes that a certain kind of experience, x, has intrinsic value, and thus desires to obtain x. But at the same time he has had experiences of this kind, and has abhorred them because of the experience in itself, not because of some effect it produces or anything else. His desires seem to be in conflict: he wants x as an instance of intrinsically valuable experiences; and he shuns it in itself. If he can by his own actions either bring about or prevent his experience of x, he must decide which desire is the stronger one. Either he brings himself to like what he believes has intrinsic value, i.e. x, or he ignores what he

believe that x is intrinsically valuable, and so forth. I presuppose e.g. that it is possible that we can want the good of other beings, since otherwise most ethics, except perhaps some forms of ethical egoism will be obsolete. As a matter of fact not even ethical egoism seems to come out better if it is true that we cannot but try to maximize our own good, since it seems pointless to say that we ought to do what we cannot avoid doing. Cf Österberg 1986.

[6] Cf John Harsanyi: "For, after all, *what* way do I myself want to be treated? To this question the fundamental answer – the only answer necessarily true, because tautologically true – is: 'I want to be treated in accordance with my own wants.'" (Harsanyi 1976, 31.)

believes to have intrinsic value. In the end he does what he most wants to do.

When someone else is to do something for this man as far as experiencing x is concerned, I find it most reasonable that he must take into consideration the desires of the man who will have the experience: if this man's abhorrence of x is the preponderant one, the desire that would determine his own actions, this ought also to be decisive for others. At least if we ought to bring about valuable states or as great a surplus of positive value over disvalue as possible. If you have a friend whom you want to be nice to, then you ought to satisfy his desires, not to maximize his sum of intrinsic value (if these two are distinct). The well-considered desires of someone express her own autonomous individuality, which we ought to respect.

Therefore nothing that is not desired for its own sake can have intrinsic value in a normatively interesting sense. But it could be the case, as several hedonists have thought, that being desired for its own sake is just a necessary condition of intrinsic value. Derek Parfit claims (1984, 502) that a possible position is that being desired is a necessary condition of having intrinsic value, but that there are other conditions that must also obtain, e.g. that the desire is in accordance with reason. This is also according to Parfit the position of Sidgwick (Parfit 1984, 500). To be desired in accordance with reason a state must have certain objective characteristics. But the examples I have seen do not convince me that we need any objective restrictions; it seems more probable that we project our own desires onto certain states and proclaim these states, desired by us, to be objectively valuable.

Is it, however, really possible that any state desired by someone for its own sake is intrinsically valuable? We can evaluate desires. It is bad to have too egotistical wants, to want to make other people suffer, to want power over others, and so forth. If we keep to Hume's guillotine we can therefore ask: is it a good thing that we have the desires that we do have? In short, are the desires we have good desires? Suppose that among the desires (of all human beings, or of a certain group of people) are desires for making other beings suffer. Are we really to accept that it is intrinsically valuable to a sadist to torture his fellow beings? I would say yes. But is it good that there are sadists (or that some are sadists, which amounts to the same)? I believe that a better formulation of the question would be: "Is it good for the victims of the sadist that the latter has sadistic impulses and satisfies them?" The answer to this question is of course no (at least as long as the victims are not masochists). This does not mean that I am a value relativist in any interesting sense. Some states are valuable to Peterson and some other to Jonson, but to both the important thing is that their desires are satisfied.

Another argument against the proposal that whatever is intrinsically desired is intrinsically valuable is the following: some may want Manchester United to win the league for its own sake, others equally hotly desire the victory for Liverpool. Is the victory of Liverpool both intrinsically good and intrinsically neutral (or even intrinsically bad)? Well, as far as I can see, the most reasonable position to overcome this difficulty is to take intrinsic value to be a relation. Something is intrinsically valuable to someone. To the Liverpool fan, the victory of his favorite team has intrinsic value. To the fan of Manchester United it lacks intrinsic value or may even be intrinsically bad. This seems quite natural, if what is intrinsically desired is intrinsically valuable. But it also seems quite natural to take "value" to be a relational term in most contexts. That instrumental value is a relation cannot be questioned: "to have instrumental value" seems to be a three-place predicate: "something is useful for P to attain the goal x". And I can see no reason why intrinsic value should not be considered as a relation too, but in this case a two-place relation: "x is intrinsically valuable to P". As a matter of fact I cannot conceive the meaning of a phrase like: "X has intrinsic value, period."

Someone might object that I am confusing genuine evaluative statements of the type "x is intrinsically valuable" with non-genuine evaluations, i.e. statements which rather report evaluations than state them – in other words the sentence "x is intrinsically valuable to P" is taken to mean "P believes that x is intrinsically valuable". But this is not what I have in mind; when I say that x is intrinsically valuable to P, I mean that x really is valuable to P. To be valuable is to be valuable to someone. Nothing can be valuable in and for itself, so to say. If you rejoin that this is what the idea of intrinsic value amounts to, then I am willing to drop the concept of intrinsic value; in that case I cannot grasp its meaning; I do not believe that anything has such an extraordinary queer quality. (Cf Mackie 1977.) I therefore believe that we can get along quite well without postulating that anything has intrinsic value.

The thesis that "intrinsically desired" can replace "intrinsically valuable" can be interpreted in two different ways. In a weak sense the thesis just maintains that what has intrinsic value is satisfaction of desire (suitably qualified). The strong interpretation connects intrinsically valuable states with what ought to be done. This is not an innocuous step, as some philosophers, notably G.E. Moore (in *Principia Ethica*), have believed. The step from "is valuable" to "ought to be" is no less problematic than the step from "is" to "ought".[7] I believe that "maximize intrinsic value" is not trivially the answer to the question "What ought we to do?" as some authors seem to have taken for granted. Several different norms can be formulated on the basis of the same assumptions about intrinsic value e.g.: "Maximize the net surplus of intrinsic positive value over intrinsic negative value!" – "Minimize intrinsic negative value!" – "See to it that the necessary conditions obtain for achieving as great a surplus of intrinsic positive value over intrinsic negative value as possible!" etc. Therefore the central problem of ethics – what should we do? – is not answered by a statement about intrinsic value. As this last question seems to me the central one in ethics, I will try to outline the connection between interests and norms and I maintain that my idea of being intrinsically desired is to be interpreted as having normative implications, but only indirectly. The connection is hinted at in the next section of this chapter and more fully spelled out in Ch. 6.

Of course there are lots of problems already with this replacement of 'intrinsic value', such as: is it really plausible to maintain that a man's life can be improved by unperceived satisfaction of desires? Are all desires on the same footing when it comes to moral relevance? And so forth. But I leave these problems to Ch. 4, since I want to state the main theses to be defended in this essay in a condensed form in this chapter and briefly outline the argument which will be more fully spelled out in the chapters to follow.

Needs are more important than desires

The second part of my main thesis says that living beings also have interests in the necessary conditions of their desire fulfillment, namely the interest that these necessary conditions obtain. And these interests are more important from the moral point of view. This last idea is the more controversial, since it makes instrumental interests more vital than intrinsic ones. Intrinsic interests are reasons for action when one's own interests are concerned. The intrinsic desires of others are only indirectly relevant: we must respect others' rights to need-satisfaction; but there is no general obligation to maximize desire-satisfaction.

The basic idea is that some interests are more central than others: by killing someone, for instance, you deprive her of everything that can

---

[7] Cf C.I. Lewis: "The problem which delimits the field of ethics is not that of the empirically good or valuable but that of the right and morally imperative." (Lewis 1950, 552) Also cf Lewis 1955, 58-77.

have value to her (at least if no Paradise is waiting for her in the life hereafter). The most basic interest of every individual is to go on living, as long as her life will not be worse than being dead. This in itself does not give a sufficient reason to accept a norm stating that the satisfaction of needs always take precedence over the satisfaction of desires. What is needed is an argument to the effect that each individual is so important that the frustration of her needs cannot be outweighed by the greater satisfaction of desires for others.

But the fact that each individual must satisfy her needs brings us somewhat nearer an understanding of the element of necessity in moral obligation.

Furthermore the importance of human autonomy explains why the prerequisites for desire-satisfaction are more important that actual satisfaction: the important thing is to safeguard the possibility of striving and acting.

To achieve any satisfaction of desire, some necessary conditions of an acceptable life must obtain. In what follows I will argue that we have (basic) needs for those things that are necessary, and in the situation sufficient, for an acceptable life (or for the means to minimize suffering, if we cannot have a minimally acceptable life). A more detailed analysis of this concept of 'need' is spelled out in Ch. 5. All values in the last analysis are based directly or indirectly on attitudes (desires, likes and dislikes, and suchlike) but our most fundamental interest is that our basic needs are satisfied, simply because this is necessary for any value at all to be realized for us.[8]

If we emphasize the importance of needs we can see one connection between values and norms more clearly. A central problem in the analysis of norms has been the question: when do we have a good reason for acting? Irrespective of whether you analyse norms as imperatives, expressions of emotion, statements of facts, or whatever, I believe that one basic question is: what does it amount to, to have a reason for acting?[9]

---

[8] Many philosophers have observed the fact that death and suffering are more morally urgent than is the satisfaction of desire (or what else is taken to have intrinsic value). See for instance Karl Popper 1945, Ch. 5 note 6, Ch. 9 note 2, and Knut Erik Tranøy, 1967.

[9] Derek Parfit maintains that we often have reasons for actions, indeed, that we know that we have such reasons: "...there are some true claims about reasons for acting..." (Parfit 1984, 452) "We know that there are reasons for acting, and that some reasons are better than others." (Parfit 1984, ix)

Reasons for acting are usually taken to consist of two elements: in the psychological sense a reason is taken to consist of one or more cognitive beliefs about the situation, the agent and the causal relationships between a possible action and the rest of the world, and some conative attitudes, wants, desires or suchlike. In an objective sense – reason is considered as something that justifies an action or a choice – the two elements are on the one side a true description of the situation, etc., and on the other side some normatively recommended goal. The two can be considered two sides of the same coin: you could maintain that the objective sense is the primary one, and take subjective reasons to be beliefs about objective reasons. Or you could do the opposite, seeing the subjective reasons as primary and seeing the belief in objective reasons merely a projection of your own subjective reasons onto the world, believing that your own preferences indicate objective reasons in the world. But of course it is possible to distinguish between the two elements and maintain that there are true descriptions of the world and its causal connections, but that there are only subjective values.[10] My main interest is in reasons of the mixed type, consisting of true descriptions and subjective goals, since I believe that all goals are subjective in the sense explained above.

Giving advice very often consists in giving reasons for acting in this sense: when someone asks you if he ought to change occupation, if he ought to sell his boat or if he ought to try to get a divorce, you very often seem to be in the position to give advice, provided you know the other person fairly well, i.e. you know his situation, his preferences and so forth. In such situations there seem to be no more severe problems than the usual (whether you can have knowledge about causal connections, about the desires of your friend, etc.). That is, this is true as long as you are required to give your advice based on the subjective interests of your friend. Such pieces of advice are, following Kant, called hypothetical, technical or pragmatic imperatives. (Kant distinguishes between these three, but these distinctions do not matter in this context.) To me it does not seem problematic to maintain that some such technical imperatives are true and even testable and that others are false: if the recommended action leads to the desired goal, then

---

[10] The converse position seems more difficult to maintain, that there are objective values but no true descriptions, since if there are objectively valuable states, this seems to presuppose that you can truly describe them as valuable, and then it seems as if there were no reasons not to accept that there can be true descriptions also of causal connections.

it is true, otherwise false.

Such advice is nearly related to *practical syllogisms* which have been discussed at least since the time of Aristotle. When used in explanations of actions – as e.g. in *Explanation and Understanding* 1971 by G.H. von Wright – the conclusion is sometimes taken to be an action. But in this context, when we are to find what a good reason for acting is, it is more natural to take the conclusion to be a norm: P ought to perform the action *a*. The paradigm of a practical syllogism then would run something like this:

P wants to realize *x*. (*X* is a state desired by P.)
Unless P performs *a*, *x* will not be realized.
Therefore: P ought to perform *a*.

It is easy to see that the conclusion does not logically follow from the premises unless "ought" is given a very special meaning – e.g. "is necessary to obtain one's goal". I believe however that this is not an unusual meaning in some contexts, e.g."You ought to take a reef in when the wind is more than 6 Beaufort". The second premiss states that the action *a* is a necessary means to attaining the goal *x*. The reason why it must be a necessary means is of course, that if it were a sufficient means to *x*, P would not have to perform *a* to obtain *x*: there could be other, perhaps better, ways to the goal. But if the action is necessary, then it must be performed, or else the goal will not be realized. Many philosophers have observed the close parallels between 'ought' and 'must'. The idea of necessary means makes the idea intelligible.[11]

That the action *a* is a necessary means to obtaining the desired goal *x* is, however, a conclusive reason for performing *a* only under at least two further conditions. First there must not exist even stronger reasons for not performing *a*. Such reasons could be for instance that the performing of *a* prevents P from obtaining an even more desired goal.

[11] Anthony Kenny argues that practical syllogisms ought to be formulated in terms of sufficient conditions of obtaining one's goals (Kenny 1975, 70-96). But he does not convince me of the truth of his position. If an action *a* leads to a goal I have, but a different action, *b*, also leads to the same goal, I must have a further reason to choose between the two. The further reasons will be something like this: both *b* and *a* lead to my goal, but there is some other goals which I want to obtain also; and to obtain these goals I have to perform *a* rather than *b*. Only in this case do I have conclusive reasons to choose *a* rather than *b*.

Secondly there must be some prospects that x will be realized if a is performed. If a is necessary to obtain x, but x nevertheless as a matter of fact never is realized, then P after all has no reason to perform a. But if these two conditions obtain, the statement that it is necessary to perform a, if x is to be realized, seems to state a good reason for P for performing a. So a sound reason for acting states that a certain action is necessary and in the situation sufficient for obtaining a desired goal, and no more important interests will be frustrated, if the action is performed. Thus it seems that in certain contexts questions about good reasons for acting can be given definite and true answers.

So far we have only considered reasons from a subjective (or egotistical) point of view. Can I not have a reason to perform an action (or to abstain from it) because it exerts an influence on the goals and interests of someone else? Let's say that I have subjective reasons to perform an action if it fulfils the conditions hitherto stated.

As 'needs' and 'desires' are distinguished in this essay it is evident that most people usually have good, subjective reasons to satisfy their needs. That statements about needs have a special standing depends upon the fact that you usually don't have to carry through any investigations concerning which goals are desired, to be able to establish that needs ought to be satisfied: they must be satisfied to obtain almost all goals. To be able to experience anything positively good, it is necessary to be alive. But it is true only in a weak sense that I must be alive at some time to be able to experience something good. A stronger version would yield that for every individual P and every point of time, t, it is true that continued existence at t is the most important interest of P. But this is not true: there are life situations and prospects of life which make it better for P to be dead. If the pessimist is right, all lives are like that. But if this is true, whether in a specific case or generally, either the specific individual or all of us need to die. If the prospects of continued existence just means that we will experience unbearable suffering, and nothing can be done about it, then we need the means to shorten life, or at least to become unconscious. Thus in most situations we must first see to it that our needs are satisfied.

Admittedly I can be prepared to risk my life in order to meet my beloved (like Romeo) or to sacrifice it to save my country or whatever. Furthermore some of our desires might be directed towards states after our death, so it is not always true that I need to stay alive to realize my desires. The converse is also possible: although my life prospects are horrible, I want to continue to exist until I have performed a certain task or until I have met my beloved once more. This means that in some situations I can have a personal project that is so important to me, that

I am prepared to sacrifice my need-satisfaction to obtain my goal. I will call such a project a "personal project". But in most situations it is true that we have good reasons to see to it that our needs are satisfied, but which our needs are depends upon the situation.

The question of when a person does have a conclusive reason for acting – in the sense that she morally ought to perform a certain action – has not as yet been answered, because there can be conflicts between the needs and desires of different individuals, and because it is conceivable that there are morally relevant factors that do not concern means / ends. However, in what follows I will presuppose that there are no other morally relevant considerations than those concerning means to desired ends. I have seen no convincing arguments that other considerations should be relevant as far as the moral status of actions is concerned. Although other considerations can be relevant when it comes to praise or blame agents or to other kinds of moral statements, I will not go into those problems here. It is possible that other factors than the consequences can be of relevance to the moral appraisal of actions, but I will presuppose without argumentation that this is not the case. This means that I accept a general teleological framework of ethics.

This does not imply that the question about which actions are morally right (obligatory), will automatically receive an answer. The reason is that an action, which I have a good subjective reason to perform, can prevent the satisfaction of some more important interest of some other individual. Subjective reasons for acting are not the only reasons there are. Moral reasons tell us what to do all things considered. And I do not believe that a consequentialist must be a maximalist: the distribution of satisfaction can be of importance. Desires and needs of different individuals can conflict. An unsatisfied need always gives rise to a reason for acting, as likewise does every unsatisfied desire. But since not all desires and needs can be met at the same time, we must have a principle for solving conflicts. As long as we do not have such a principle, the question about what makes an action morally obligatory, has no answer. Thus far we have only stated what it is to have a good or conclusive subjective reason for acting. We can say that we have provided a sketch of a principle of prudence. But this is not the same as a principle of morals.

I have presupposed that no other considerations than those of means / ends are morally relevant. I have further argued that if anything is intrinsically good it is desire-satisfaction. But I have also proposed that need-satisfaction is more important for each individual, since if his needs are frustrated, most of his desires will also be frustrated. Now the problem is which solution is the correct one of the problem of distribution of the means to satisfaction of needs and desires. A straighforward preference utilitarian would argue that there is no problem of distribution: the sum of desire-satisfaction is what counts. You could argue that the best distribution is the one that maximizes satisfaction, if "intrinsically valuable" is the same as "intrinsically desired", then each part of the sum of satisfaction is desired by someone, a greater sum is more desired than a smaller, and hence more valuable. But this is not so, no one desires the sum of satisfaction. And I am – as I have already stated – not convinced that straight maximizing is the only reasonable answer to the question "What ought we to do?"

On the other hand I am also sceptical towards the possibility of establishing some principle of distribution as objectively true beyond doubt. My reasons are briefly the following. It is difficult to grasp what it would be like for a normative principle of just distribution to be objectively true. Such a truth must either be established as a logical truth or as corresponding to facts or as cohering with other firmly held beliefs in a reflective equilibrium. It does not seem probable that such a principle would be a logical truth; besides it seems difficult to understand how a logical truth could generate substantial norms. It is also difficult to imagine that there are some normative facts for such a principle to correspond to. This assumption would make our conception of the world more complex than necessary – since it presupposes that beside "ordinary" facts there are a special kind of "normative facts".

The coherence view of moral knowledge seems to imply that we had better conceive moral statements as statements about some natural facts, e.g. sociological or psychological facts, since this would make our bulk of convictions more consistent than if we presuppose that moral statements are quite different from statements of fact, *sui generis* so to say. Therefore it seems to me desirable to try to make moral statements part and parcel of our ordinary web of beliefs. I will try to make probable that some ultimate moral principles can be viewed as principles that we would have good subjective reasons to try to establish as social rules. This would explain the methods traditionally used in moral philosophy without making extravagant epistemological or ontological assumptions. The methods used in moral philosophy boil down after all to someone proposing some norm or principle and inviting others to consider his proposal: is this not what you believe is right too? Now it is usual to believe that what such a proposal is to be tested against is the intuitions of one's peers. But do we really have to believe that these intuitions give us a true picture of a normative reality? Since they often diverge, at least not all of them can express true insights. It seems to me more reasonable to believe that at least some of these intuitions are expressions of prejudices or likes and dislikes, which we project onto the world. I propose that instead we try to view moral principles as conventions which we have good reasons to try to get accepted, and that we try to find out how far such a conception of ethics can bring us towards a clear view of the nature and validity of ethical statements. (Cf Mackie 1977.) If we could explain in a satisfactory way very generally shared ethical convictions as natural expressions of principles which we have good subjective reasons to have generally accepted, then much would have been gained when it comes to interpreting, validating, and justifying ethical statements.[12]

All human beings – perhaps all living beings – are dependent on others. Robinson Crusoe can exist just for a short time. Our uniquely long and exposed infancy makes us vulnerable. When we grow old we usually have to be taken care of. Between childhood and old age we are in countless ways dependent upon each other to get our needs satisfied. In short we need the help from others. This presupposes either that we force others to help us or that we agree about principles for solving conflicts and of mutual aid. We have a vital interest to come to terms with at least some people, since no one is strong enough to enforce the help of others on his own. *Leviathan* 1651 by Hobbes, *Varieties of Goodness* 1963 by von Wright, and *Morals by Agreement* 1986 by Gauthier are just a few of the books from diverse times that have pleaded similar theories about the origin of morals.

Since each of us has a good reason to defend the satisfaction of our own needs, our primary interest must be to see to it that this will be guaranteed. It is true that I can imagine some situation where I would be willing to sacrifice my life in order to realize a dream, and this might be true of you too. But you are hardly willing to sacrifice your life in order

---

[12] I will not go further into the intricate problems of meta-ethics in this context, since this essay is not intended to be a treatment of those questions. This sketch (partly inspired by Ch. X of G.H.von Wright's *Varieties of Goodness* and by J.L. Mackie, *Ethics. Inventing Right and Wrong*) is just intended to give some idea of the structure of the argument in Ch. 6, where I will argue that we have good subjective reasons to try to establish certain principles as social conventions. If you disagree with me on the questions of the status and interpretation of ethical statements, you can just compare your own intuitions with my proposals. If you agree with the main normative conclusions, ask yourself why you want to keep to a more complicated view of the normative reality than necessary. If you disagree, show me what intuitions come into conflict with my principles and why your intutions are to be trusted.

to let my dream come true, and *vice versa*. Thus we would agree that no one's satisfaction of needs would be sacrificed in order to satisfy the desires or realize the personal projects of others. At the same time we would hardly be prepared to forego satisfaction of desires to save our own lives or those of others, unless these lives were worth living: you have a conclusive reason to satisfy your needs only as long as you have some prospects of living a decent life.

Lastly it seems not very likely that we could come to an agreement about how much help we are to give each other when it comes to satisfying our desires. Certainly a lot of satisfaction could be brought about if we all strove to maximize the total sum of satisfactions, but at the same time a rule to that effect could mean that we might be forced to sacrifice our own satisfaction for the end of the greater satisfaction of others. Some might therefore argue that we ought to strive for as equal a distribution as possible of satisfactions, others would plead the maximization strategy, still others would give their vote for other principles. The minimal rule that could win unanimous adherence is probably that we should not interfere with the strivings of each other, as long as these strivings do not conflict.

Isn't this a void prescript? If I interfere with your strivings, then our desires do conflict; so I will not go against the norm, if this is not stated in a more precise way. Let us distinguish between those desires which directly concern one's own life and those that do not. Then only those desires which directly concern one's own life must conflict to justify an interference. But how are we to draw the line between those desires which directly concern my own life and those that do not? I will discuss this question more fully in Ch. 4. Just to indicate the result: my desire not to live in a world where some people experience pleasure from inflicting pain on others is not sufficient to justify my interference with sado-masochistic practices among consenting adults. But if some sadist wants to flog me, our conflict of interest is such as to justify interference.

The idea that we ought to leave people to strive for their own goals is further strengthened by the conception of human beings as autonomous persons: the best life for such an individual is a life where she herself tries to reach her goals. This explains why respect is more important than maximizing and why the prerequisites of a good life should be considered more important than maximal desire-satisfaction.

In brief we all have good subjective reasons to try to come to an agreement with other people about a "moral system", i.e. a system of conventional rules which are rather similar to those which many take to be transcendentally valid moral rules. The reason why we have such reasons is that we cannot satisfy our needs and desires on our own. The "moral system" I propose therefore is not a moral system valid for all rational being – if e.g. angels are rational but incorporeal and they lack other needs, they would have no subjective reasons for coming to an agreement on moral rules of this kind. Animals cannot agree on rules because they lack language but they certainly do have needs. Therefore we can understand that they have interests and can decide to take their needs and desires into consideration also.

However, we need not reach an agreement with all living beings to live according to certain rules, as long as the group of people living according to them is big enough to satisfy the needs of the members of the group. At least this is true as long as the communications and connections with other groups are few or non-existent. But I believe that the integration of the modern world, ecologically, economically, politically, and militarily, makes the need for a global system of rules more and more urgent.[13]

Suppose that some people or groups of people refuse to accept to respect any reciprocal rights, because they are strong enough to defend their own interests. They decline for instance to forsake the satisfaction of their own desires in order to satisfy the needs of others. As a matter of fact this is the possible world which is also actual. Are not these people simply acting wrongly? Of course they are: and the rules of the system sketched above say just that. Other people – especially those whose interests are sacrificed – condemn such behaviour. In severe cases we even punish such behaviour. In brief they act wrongly. It might be true that such persons have no subjective reasons to adhere to the rules of the system. But this just means that in such situations self-interest conflicts with morals. (Which rules will be included in such a system I will try to make plausible in Ch. 6).

The important thing is not so much acceptance but what we have reasons to try to get accepted. The idea is that we all have interests to safeguard, but we cannot get all our interests maximally satisfied without losses for other individuals. And we cannot get guarantees for the satisfaction of our important interests without offering the same guarantees for others. But of course the rich part of the world can unite

---

[13] As far back as in the middle of the 17th century the lives of the bushmen in South Africa were influenced by actions by the Inuits living in Greenland, if we can trust an article in *Dagens Nyheter*, 12 July 1990: "Ett sälsamt samband". By preparing the skins from seals better than did the Dutch hunters from South Africa, the latter's trade with seal skin was diminished, and more seals were left for bushmen's household hunt.

against the poor part. The slaveholders united against the slaves in ancient Greece as well as in the Southern states of the USA in the 19th century. My idea is that although the common conventions in these states allowed the slave system, this was not accepted by the slaves, or even if it had been accepted among a large part of the slave population, they would not have accepted it, had they been fully informed. The slaves therefore had legitimate claims which can be considered as "moral claims", i.e. claims which they wanted acknowledged and satisfied, although they were not socially acknowledged by the upper classes. Thus there were social claims that the slaveholders were to respect the autonomy of the slaves (which would mean the abolition of slavery). As long as the slaveholders were strong enough to keep the slaves down, they had no subjective reasons to accept the claims, but the claims were nonetheless real and the slaves had sound reasons for their claims. Since also the whites in the USA and the free Greeks had reasons to claim freedom, there were in my sense moral claims requiring the abolitions of slavery, although these claims were not acknowledged. All human beings have sound reasons to claim freedom and this is what makes them legitimate.

What I need, strictly speaking, is that others respect these rules as far as my interests are concerned. I would gain if others respected my rights, but I myself could escape the claims of others. Hence the tension between self-interest and morality, i.e. the social conventions just sketched. Therefore sanctions are tied to rule-breaking: disapproval, decreased help from others, in grave cases punishment and so forth. The sanctions are intended to make sure that the offender loses more than he gains from breaking the rules. But all gain in the long run from having a system of rules rather than being without it. At least no one loses very much (her life e.g.) and most people gain a lot – those who do not gain on the system in the long run are those that could have satisfied a lot more desires if they had not foregone their own satisfaction in order that others could satisfy their vital needs. So if you can avoid being detected and at the same time gain from breaking the rules, then you do not have a subjective reason to keep to the rules. However, since most of the time we all gain from the rules being in force, we try to foster feelings of guilt in those who break the rules, we try to implement the rules in our offspring, try to make it desirable to be known as an honest person and undesirable to be known as a scoundrel, etc.

A more problematic objection to this conception of morals seems to be the following: suppose that it is necessary if the great majority of people are to obtain great satisfaction of their desires, that they sacrifice the satisfaction of the basic needs for some individual(s). Wouldn't the social contract sanction that? Minorities could come off very badly if the contract were voted through by a ruthless majority. Therefore I have advocated unanimous consensus (or something very close to it). But what is the justification of that, if not some moral intuition to the effect that no single individual is to be sacrificed for the common good, as long as the majority are not so badly off after all. Can there be some other motivation for requiring consensus?

One reason is that no one can be certain that he will belong to the majority. Everyone – even the strongest among us – needs protection of his most basic interests. In a situation of need we would all claim the help of others. It is this claim that in a generalized form constitutes the moral claim. A strong majority might not want to respect the moral claims. But moral claims do not always give us subjective reasons for action. Moral claims are not intrinsically motivating, I believe. The point of my analysis of morality is rather that we get a conceivable interpretation of moral norms: they express the claims everyone must put forward against all others.

My attempt to justify moral rules thus connects with the contractualist tradition. The objection against such ideas, that no contract has been entered into, and that no one can be bound by a hypothetical agreement, does not hit my version. I have not argued that we are bound by a contract – I have tried to show that we have sound subjective reasons to try to get some principles established and observed. These reasons are based on the fact that we have needs that we cannot satisfy on our own.

This is of course a rather rough sketch, which will be spelled out in more detail in what follows. In Ch. 4 I will state more fully what kinds of attitudes are morally relevant, i.e. which kinds of attitudes would we consider important to satisfy and under which conditions. In Ch. 5 the concept of 'need' is discussed. And in Ch. 6 the moral principles that follow from my conception of ethics are stated and argued for. But first I want to sketch the background of my project. My enterprise connects at two points with a main stream of Western moral philosophy: the distinction between needs and desires goes back at least to Plato. And with him, Socrates, and the Sophists this question is tied to the quest for an objective basis for ethics, among the ancient Greeks traditionally sought in human nature. The two next chapters will outline and comment on these connections.

Chapter 2

A Central Concept in Western Philosophy

In *The Republic* Plato distinguishes between necessary and unnecessary desires:

> ...in order not to argue in the dark, shall we first define our distinction between necessary and unnecessary appetites?
> – Let us do so.
> – Well, then, desires that we cannot divert or suppress may be properly called necessary, and likewise those whose satisfaction is beneficial to us, may they not? For our nature compels us to seek their satisfaction. Is not that so?
> / – – – /
> – And what of the desires from which a man could free himself by discipline from youth up, and whose presence in the soul does no good and in some cases harm? Should we not fairly call all such unnecessary?
> – Fairly indeed. (*The Republic* Book VIII 558-559, translation by P.Shorey)

The need for bread is an example of the first category, the desire for relishes belongs to the second class (if they are nourishing). Desire for luxuries is neither useful nor necessary.

As a matter of fact Plato introduces two different distinctions which will be important during the millennia to come: he not only distinguishes necessary from unnecessary desires, he also distinguishes 'what we *believe* that we desire' from 'our *true* desires' (*Gorgias* 466-467). The last-mentioned distinction of course anticipates the distinction between 'true' and 'false needs' which has played an important role in discussions in our century.

I believe that it is true to say that these distinctions form parts of a more general project of Plato's: to distinguish the true good from that which only seems good, which in turn exemplifies Plato's general philosophical project which aims at distinguishing true reality from mere appearance.

Aristotle discusses a similar division of the desires in connection with his discussion of the virtue of temperance in his *Nicomachean Ethics* (VII, iv f). He makes a tripartition of the desires: those that are necessary and connected with the functions of the body (nourishment, sex, etc.), which are good to satisfy as long as you do not indulge too much in them; those that are natural and directed towards desirable things, such as honour and wealth (these too can be excessive); and those that are unnatural and evil in themselves, such as the cannibal's lust for human flesh.

The Epicureans also divided the desires into necessary, natural, and unnatural. Cicero gives the following account of their standpoint:

> One kind /of desires/ he /Epicurus/ classified as both natural and necessary, a second as natural without being necessary, and a third as neither natural nor necessary; the principle of classification being that the necessary desires are gratified with little trouble or expense; the natural desires also require but little, since nature's own riches, which suffice to content her, are both easily procured and limited in amount; but for the imaginary desires no bound or limit can be discovered. (Cicero, *De finibus* I xiii 45, translation by H. Rackham.)

The necessary ones are according to the Epicureans the physiological needs for food, water, air and so forth. Sexual desire is an example of a natural but not necessary want. And the desire for luxury is – as usual – an example of the last category.

The Stoic Cicero finds the partition of Epicurus clumsy: you ought first to distinguish between natural and unnatural desires and then make two parts of the natural ones: the necessary ones and the unnecessary ones (*ibid.* II ix, 26). The Stoics had a different conception of human nature from that of Plato e.g.; their idea was that a good man simply didn't have the same desires as an evil man: he just had the natural ones. His desires were easily satisfied, and he therefore had his fate in his own hands. The Stoic Seneca writes in his 90th letter to Lucilius about the supreme value of a simple life, untouched by technical innovations, progress and comforts: "The things that are indispensable require no elaborate pains for their acquisition; it is only luxuries that call for labour. /.../ Follow nature..." (translation by R.M. Gummere). The Stoics and the Epicureans as well as Plato agree that it is easy and inexpensive to satisfy the needs.

One of the basic questions of ancient Greek moral philosophy was: which are the conditions for a good life? Men desire and strive for so many different things: pleasure, honour, wealth. Which wants is it really necessary to satisfy in order to live a good life? There were two kinds of answer to this question: some answers, e.g. that of Aristotle, said that it was appropriate to strive for satisfaction of some of our desires according to our nature – and to get it – since we then lived according to our nature. Some other answers, e.g. those of the Cynics, the Epicureans and the Stoics, focused the interest upon the necessary conditions of any good human life, such as the satisfaction of basic needs. These needs were of course also determined by human nature.

The frame of the moral discussion in ancient Greece was the problem of how are we to live in order to live well? In *The Acts* needs are for the first time in Western history mentioned in connection with distribution. The stress put upon equality, love, and charity by the first Christians connects the idea of needs with the problem of distributing scarce resources: "to each according to his needs". (*The Acts* 2.45. also cf Springborg 1981, 20.) In Medieval Europe it was maintained that the poor have a just claim to the surplus of the wealth of the rich. Some thinking is devoted to make clear what a person needs and what is superfluous. (E.g. Thomas Aquinas and Lyndwood (the latter of the 15th century; cf B. Tierney, 1959, 33 and 36; also cf Carlyle & Carlyle 1909.) In practice needs are taken to be relative to the social status of a person. A bishop e.g. needed 50 companions on horseback, when travelling. Nonetheless the poor man could lay a just claim on the surplus, he even had a right to steal it, if it was not given to him voluntarily.

In the 17th century the scientific breakthrough revived the discussion about human drives. New theories were formulated about human nature modelled on conceptions in contemporary physics. Hobbes and Spinoza built ethical theories on theories about innate human drives, the primary one taken to be a drive to self-maintenance. Spinoza is anxious to distinguish the desires we actually happen to have and those that are rationally justified. Only if we act on the basis of the latter desires, do we act for our own best self-interest.

The idea – although not the exact formulation – that all human beings ought to work according to their capacity and consume according to their needs was proposed in the texts of Gerrard Winstanley and practised in the social experiment at S:t George's Hill (*Law of*

Freedom, 1652).

In the 18th century Rousseau condemned modern civilization on account of its corruptive influence on man, considered to be good in the state of nature. False needs are created and cause conflicts and dissatisfaction. The dream of the simple, genuine man, "the happy savage", is again a theme of the critique of culture and civilization. Rousseau belonged to a primitivistic tradition from Lucretius (*De rerum natura*) and Seneca (cf above) who in turn were inspired by Cynical and Stoic thinking: the ideal of "a life according to nature" (cf the discussion of that maxim at the end of this chapter).

It is worth noting that the opposing of 'needs' and 'luxury' and the desirability of a frugal life was not only a part of philosophical critique of the way of living of the upper classes. Such ideas also play an important role when it comes to repressing the claims of the lower classes (and of women) to share the good things in life. Lawmakers and moralists from ancient times onwards are anxious to punish and condemn people who try to get clothes, food, and housing that are not in accordance with their social standing and conditions. Also in this context the distinction between needs and unnecessary desires plays a role. (See Sekora 1977, especially the first chapter.)

At the beginning of the 19th century Hegel formulated a theory of human needs, which seems to go against the mainstream of European thought. He denies that human nature and human needs are static, he has the opinion that human needs are the result of cultural conditioning and he assents to these culturally formed needs:

> *Das Thier* hat einen beschränkten Kreis von Mitteln und Weisen der Befriedigung seiner gleichfalls beschränkten Bedürfnisse. *Der Mensch* beweist auch in dieser Abhängigkeit zugleich sein Hinausgehen über dieselbe und seine Allgemeinheit, zunächst durch die *Vervielfältigung* der Bedürfnisse und Mittel, und dann durch *Zerlegung* und *Unterscheidung* des concreten Bedürfnisses in einzelne Theile und Seiten, welche verschiedene *partikularisierte*, damit *abstractere* Bedürfnisse werden. (Hegel, 1821, § 190)

Human nature is not something given once and for all, according to Hegel, it is formed in different ways in different historical circumstances and it gets a definite form through human history as a whole. That needs change and develop through history is nothing to complain about. On the contrary these changing needs are forces in the process of history; and the historical process is something positively valued by Hegel. When needs and the ways to satisfy them change, society also changes. But the society influences the needs. Thus there is a continual interaction between society and human needs. According to Hegel human freedom is increased through the developing needs, not the other way around as Rousseau had maintained. Since man is no longer a slave to the elementary needs like an animal, taste, fashion, and desire for variation forces man to *choose*. (*Ibid* § 194) But this freedom is just formal: in § 195 Hegel admits that the desires for luxury can also become fetters.

Socialists contemporary with Hegel, however, formulate their criticism of capitalism and modern society and their critique embodies a more traditional conception of needs. Modern society is unjust, because it makes possible the satisfaction of the increasingly artificial desires and whims of the upper classes, while it denies the majority of the people the satisfaction even of their basic needs. Mably, Morelly, Babeuf, Blanc, Fourier, Saint-Simon, Cabet, Owen, and several others consider this the fundamental problem of modern society. Morelly, Babeuf, Blanc, and Cabet all embrace the idea we have already encountered in Winstanley, that the resources of society ought to be distributed according to needs, while the members of society share the burdens of production according to their capacities. Perhaps Louis Blanc is the first one to make the idea a slogan: "Produira selon ses facultés et consommera selon ses besoins." (L. Blanc, *Organisation du Travail*, 1st ed. 1839, quoted from 9th ed. 1850, 72)[1]

Marx conjoins the Hegelian conception of historically determined needs and his positive evaluation of culturally shaped wants with the socialist criticism of the unjust distribution of the means of their satisfaction. The concept of 'need' plays a central role in the economic theory of Marx: 'use-value' is defined in terms of human needs, and no commodity has exchange-value without use-value. The value of labour is determined by the needs of the workers: the capitalist pays the workers enough to reproduce, i.e. the vital needs of the workers must be satisfied. Capital furthermore has its own needs – it must yield interest and therefore needs to be profitable. The development of the productive forces makes possible the production of surplus value, i.e. more goods are produced than necessary for the satisfaction of the needs of the workers.

Thus in the works of Marx needs play an important role as elements in explanations and theories. But they also play a role in his

---

[1] According to Patricia Springborg, Babeuf is the one who has the copyright, but I have not been able to confirm that.

evaluations, since in his vision of the communist society they are the measure of justice. (Cf Patricia Springborg 1981, 13.) According to Patricia Springborg 1981 (Ch. 1) the concept of 'need' is the link between different parts of the marxist theory: Marx' ontology, anthropology, psychology, economics, and his theory of justice – in all these parts the concept of 'need' plays a central role. In spite of this the concept of 'need' is never systematically discussed in the texts of Marx. Here and there a lot is said about needs, but less in the form of conceptual analysis than in terms of empirical statements about needs. Thus it is never clear if Marx mostly takes needs to be impulses to behaviour or to be necessary conditions of desirable ends. In different contexts he seems to presuppose different meanings.

Human needs are socially determined, Marx maintains; they are formed by society and society by the needs. The "invisible hand" of Adam Smith and the related idea of the "cunningness of Reason" of Hegel, i.e. the idea that everyone through pursuing his egotistical interests, thereby unintentionally furthers the common good, this idea is given a rather mysterious explanation in Marx: he believes that the explanation is that private interests are as a matter of fact socially determined and that society gives rise to just those needs that tend to further the progress of civilization (Marx 1903).

Marx did not believe that there is any difference between needs and desires as far as social influence is concerned. Even the most basic needs are socially determined in respect of the means preferred for their satisfaction. Cultural prejudice can make it practically impossible to satisfy a need in a way not customary to us. Even the natural ones are influenced by society; there are both natural needs historically spelled out and needs which are wholly historically determined. A natural but historically differentiated need is the need for food:

> Hunger ist Hunger, aber Hunger der sich durch gekochtes, mit Gabel und Messer gegessnes Fleisch befriedigt, ist ein andrer Hunger, als der rohes Fleisch mit Hilfe von Hand, Nagel und Zahn verschlingt. (Marx 1903. Quotation from Marx-Engels, *Werke* Bd 13, 624, Dietz Verlag, Berlin, 1972.)

'Natural needs' seem not to be a definitely determinable class of needs in the texts of Marx, rather they are some kind of a limit: unless they are satisfied life cannot be reproduced. (Cf Agnes Heller 1978, Ch. 1.) But the minimum of subsistence is also a relative concept, differing from one society to another. Production gives rise to new needs: it is only when a certain consumer commodity is obtainable that a need for it is formed (Marx 1845-46). Marx did not only reckon physiological needs as needs; there are also needs for activity and self-realization, for instance. He sometimes distinguished between true and false needs, but it is not easy to see how he did so. The distinction is anyhow not made in the same way as in Rousseau: Marx's idea is not that true needs are those of "primitive" people; rather the true needs are those that will still be needs in the communist society.

In *Das Kapital* Marx talks about abstract needs which are the same for all human beings, but when it comes to a certain individual his needs are specific and historically determined. In the same work Marx distinguishes between necessary consumer commodities (necessary according to the customs of the society concerned, not according to physiological criteria) and luxuries, which do not form a part of the normal consumption of the working classes. All class societies give rise to these two groups of consumer articles. (The question about the relativity of needs will be more discussed in Ch. 5 pp 98-101.)

In socialist society and even more in communist society the need to work will more and more become the dominant need, since you have left the "kingdom of necessity", i.e. the necessary production intended to cover the basic needs will claim less and less work and time (Marx 1875, Marx Engels, *Werke* Bd 19, 21). In the same work Marx distinguishes between two kinds of justice: one will be realized in socialist society, the second and higher one is found in communist society. It is not until communism that the old socialist slogan will be realized: "From each according to his ability, to each according to his needs!"

A basic problem in the interpretation of Marx's theory of needs, pointed out by Cornelius Castoriadis (1978) among others, is that Marx does not seem to take his own theory about the social relativity of needs seriously. He presupposes absolute, "natural", needs in some parts of his theory: the needs of the workers must be given if labour is to be a commodity with a fixed price; the needs must be delimited if the idea about abundance in communist society and the principle of social justice valid there is to be conceivable. Alienation during capitalism influences the needs of people so that means become ends and *vice versa*. In capitalist economy the satisfaction of needs – which ought to be the end – becomes a means to profit. The need to use things is replaced by the need to own them. Unless human needs are given Marx does not have the ground for questioning convention, the laws and values of society, which he must to make the communist project reasonable. If the needs are wholly socially determined, the contrast between *'nomos'* and *'physis'*, between 'convention' and 'nature' disappears. Therefore Marx in his youth is attracted by a materialistic theory of given needs. But this is successively replaced by a more dynamic theory, where needs are formed by society and society by needs. Kate Soper (1981) is of the opinion that we must keep to the idea that the needs are socially determined (Soper 1981, 20-37), and this in turn implies that we must take 'need' as a normative concept. Needs are not *given* as a basis for morality. On the contrary you must take a normative stand to decide when there is a need, according to Soper:

> ... to plan to meet needs ... is to assume political responsibility for all decisions and actions relating to production. And that, in turn, means facing, fairly and squarely, the problem of the criterion of need; it involves decisions about what is 'valuable' (needed) and therefore worth producing. (Soper 1981, 211)

Castoriadis has the opinion that we must make a normative decision on the question of which needs ought to be fostered by society.

A socially formed need under capitalism is the "radical need" to crush capitalism and transform society into socialism. Capitalism produces more and more commodities and needs while at the same time it does not satisfy these needs for the great masses. (Heller 1974, Ch. 4)

After Freud and the development of modern psychology as an independent science, the interest in human drives gains new power. Different attempts are made to establish the basic drives and needs. During some periods a reductionist tendency is dominant: all human motivation is reduced to one or a few basic drives, sometimes called "instincts", sometimes "needs", sometimes something else. The term "need" is popular in the 30s and 40s, in the work of Henry A. Murray and Clark L. Hull, for instance. In the 50s Abraham Maslow constructs his famous hierarchy of needs. In the 60s Erich Fromm and Herbert Marcuse criticize modern society because of its inability to foster and satisfy "true human needs".[2] Fromm and Marcuse are both influenced by Freud but also by Marx. But in opposition to the latter they do not believe that capitalism fosters a "radical need" for change; rather they are of the opinion that it forms within its members *false needs*, such that lend themselves to satisfaction within the frame of capitalism.They will therefore tend to reproduce and prolong capitalism. Fromm and Marcuse thus introduce a distinction between "true" and "false needs" which will be important in the critique of the developed societies in the Western world in the 20th century.

---

[2] Maslow and Marcuse are dicussed a little more in the next chapter.

Jean-Paul Sartre treats in *Critique de la raison dialectique* (1960) "besoin" as a central concept, which he wants to fulfill the double aim of making possible explanations of human actions and saving the ontological freedom Sartre had defended in *L'etre et le néant* (1943). When Sartre replaces 'desire' from *L'etre et le néant* by 'need' in *Critique* he refers to Hegel and Marx. But at the same time he tries to save something from his own theory of human freedom. 'Need' is connected with 'scarcity', which to Sartre both is a contingent fact – some people are hungry and feel cold – and a more metaphysical, absolute state – there are always desires that are not satisfied. (Cf Springborg 1981, 131.) Since "scarcity" (like "need") refers to a "negative fact", that something is missing, Sartre still can maintain that man himself creates his needs and his scarcity: that something is *missing* is not an "objective" fact of the world. Thereby freedom is saved at the same time as Sartre tries to make possible the historical explanations of Hegel and Marx.

In the 1970s, satisfaction of basic needs succeeded increased equality as a goal of development strategies for the poorest countries of the world. Before increased equality the goal had been economic growth in terms of increased GNP (see for example J. McHale and M.C. McHale, 1978 and Paul Streeten et al. 1981.)

> During three years of sudden conceptual change, from 1974 to 1977, national development strategies, international negotiations and global organizations have begun to be deeply affected by the simple notion that the purpose of economic development and international cooperation is to meet the human requirements of people, and especially the minimum needs of the neediest. (McHale & McHale 1978, 3)

In the 80s, this idea was in turn replaced by the goal adjustment to the world market, as is well known. But now in the 80s and 90s needs are discussed in the contexts of the limited resources of nature. Increased production will ultimately make human life on earth impossible. Therefore it is important to try to decide what we really need and what could reasonably be characterized as luxuries: see William Leiss 1978. Leiss does not try to distinguish between "natural" or "true needs" on the one hand and "culturally determined needs" on the other. All needs, according to Leiss, are culturally formed, when it comes to concrete goals of human strivings. In spite of this he is worried about the limits conferred on satisfaction of human needs by the scarcity of natural resources and the actual forms of needs in modern society. Another author working on the same lines is Ivan Illitch. But he belongs rather in the primitivistic tradition from Rousseau and the Stoics.[3]

Problems: interests rooted in human nature

When Western moral philosophers have striven to distinguish necessary from unnecessary desires their motives have been mixed: some of them wanted to praise the frugal life as superior to a life in luxury, others have been indignant with unjust distribution, still others have been interested in finding a basis of morality in human nature. One question that comes to mind is whether these different ideas and distinctions really have anything in common? Is there some kind of kinship between the different attempts at distinguishing between "necessary" and "unnecessary desires", "true" and "false needs", "needs" and "desires" and so forth? I believe there is. The proposed distinctions are all attempts to classify interests into important and less important ones. And the distinctions are in one way or another based on ideas about which interests are rooted in human nature and which are not. But there are two different ways of making the distinction: one idea is that some interests have to be satisfied because they are determined by our nature, they are so to say true expressions of our nature, they are natural, not conventional. The other idea boils down to this: some conditions are necessary to any good life. Of course which these conditions are also depends on our natural constitution. But nonetheless there is a significant difference between these two ideas. In this book I have tried to follow up both ideas and also to make clear the links between the two.

Ever since the Sophists introduced the distinction between conventional morals and objectively valid morals, attempts have been made again and again in European moral philosophy to base morality upon human nature. If there are objectively valid moral norms they must, at least in part be determined by facts about human beings. A.O. Lovejoy and G. Boas have with their usual thoroughness laid bare the roots of the idea of nature as norm in ancient Greece in *Primitivism and Related Ideas in Antiquity* (1935, new edition 1965; references to the last-mentioned edition.)

The Sophists of ancient Greece were the first ones known to us who attached ideas about an objectively valid ethics to theories about a

---

[3] Cf e.g. "Useful Unemployment and Its Professional Enemies", *Towards a History of Needs,* Pantheon, New York 1977.

human nature common to all men. Through their occupation – they taught rhetoric, which equipped men in the Greek democratic societies to win success in political, legal, and personal affairs – they became aware of the differences between groups and societies concerning culture, conventions, and morals. Thereby the question was raised of whether morals could possibly be a non-conventional matter. Many Sophists, for example Protagoras, Gorgias, and Polos (in the Platonic dialogue *Gorgias*) were of the opinion that no objective morals existed, all moral judgements merely expressed the conventional views of society. Other Sophists, like e.g. Antiphon, Hippias, and Antisthenes (as a pupil not only of Gorgias but also of Socrates he is sometimes not considered as a Sophist), insisted that you have to distinguish what is considered right and good according to convention from what is right and good according to nature. In this connection they thought that in particular human nature must be the norm: the way human beings in fact are constituted, their true needs and potentialities must be the basis of morality. It is probable that they formed their theories about human nature under influence from contemporary theories in medicine. (See Jaeger 1934) This path was continued, broadened, and deepened by Socrates, Plato, and Aristotle.

Lovejoy and Boas express their regret that the Sophists formulated their question about the possibility of an objectively valid ethics in terms of *"physis"* ("nature") a notoriously ambiguous term in the Greek language. Boas and Lovejoy distinguishes 66 different interpretations of the term, which they classify in 9 main groups:

(a) That which anything is 'by nature' as its intrinsic or objective character, in contrast with subjective appearances or with human beliefs about it – an antithesis applied first to the objects of the external world /.../.

(b) 'Nature' in contrast with 'law', 'custom' or 'convention', as the objectively valid in the realm of morals, existing positive law or custom being assumed to deviate from this objective standard partially or completely /.../.

(c) That which is true or valid 'by nature' as what is universally known to or accepted by mankind, in contrast with beliefs or standards peculiar to particular nations, periods or individuals – an interpretation of the criterion of objective validity implied by (b) /.../.

(d) 'Nature' as the general cosmic order, optimistically conceived as good, or as divinely ordained, in contrast with supposed deviations from this order arising from human error or depravity – 'Nature' in

this sense tending from an early period to be more or less vaguely personified /.../.
(e) The 'natural' state of a living being as its healthy condition, in contrast with conditions of disease or impairment of functions – a sense already common in the Hippocratic writings /.../.
(f) The 'natural' state of any being as its congenital or original condition; hence, in the case of mankind, or of a given people, its primeval state, in contrast with subsequent historic alterations or accretions /.../.
(g) 'Nature' as that which exists apart from man and without human effort or contrivance, in contrast with 'art', i.e. with all that is artificial or man-made /.../.
(h) 'Nature' as that *in* man which is not due to taking thought or to deliberate choice: hence, those modes of human desire, emotion, or behavior which are instinctive or spontaneous, in contrast with those which are due to the laboring intellect, to premeditation, to self-consciousness, or to instruction /.../.
(i) The 'natural' state of human life as that in which the only government is that of the family or the patriarchal clan, in contrast with that in which there exist formal and 'artificial' political institutions and laws /.../. (Lovejoy and Boas 1965, 12-13)

Which interpretation seems the most promising? To me it seems as if some combination of the ideas in (a), (b), and (e) could be developed into a credible standpoint as far as morals are concerned. Some aspects of the idea that our natural properties determine what we ought to do, are rather trivial. No one would deny for instance that what is nourishing is determined by characteristics of our digestion; that we ought to sleep for some hours each twenty-four hours because of our physiological constitution; that we ought not to shun all kinds of bodily movement; and so forth. Likewise some kinds of activity are more in accordance with our nature than are others: very one-sided manual work will harm the body, and mental stress will under some conditions result in illness and suffering. What constitutes a healthy life is thus determined to a great extent by our nature in a rather trivial sense. The problem is not to oscillate between those interpretations of the principle of living according to nature which are trivial and those which are not. The question is whether or not this is what is done when we maintain that nature is the norm even in moral contexts.

The Sophists, Socrates, and Aristotle broaden the analogy to be valid for determining what is a good human life on the whole. Very general rules could, they thought, be formulated based on the common human constitution. This was the only question of interest to Socrates and Aristotle, since they were convinced that human nature was relatively determinate, and that what was of importance was attaining the excellence specific to the species to which one belongs. This is an expression of the conceptual realism of Socrates: the idea (form) of man determines what constitutes a *good* man; what is important is that each man is as good a specimen of the human species as possible in much the same way as the best knife is that which satisfies the defining characteristics of a knife as much as possible.

Aristotle attempts to base morals on human nature by developing the Socratic notion that man has a function and that to perform this function well is to live well. To live in accordance with his nature means, according to Aristotle, to lead a life where those characteristics specific to his species are maximally realized. If you are a man, the best life is the most human one, i.e. the characteristics specific to human beings are maximally developed. Since reason is what distinguishes man, according to the opinion of Aristotle, the best life for man is the most rational life, a life dedicated to rational activity − scientific research and philosophy first and foremost − governed by rational rules. The best man is he who by exercise has acquired habits and dispositions to act and react rationally in all kinds of situations.

But you could ask why the species-specific characteristics are the ones that ought to be developed maximally? General advice concerning nourishing food is valid for most human beings. But more specific rules apply to certain individuals. Thus the diabetic needs extra insulin to survive. In an analogous way you could suppose that a good human life in general ought to be adapted to general human characteristics, but be modified in concrete circumstances by the specific characteristics of the specific individual. If a person is not very rational, but has certain other potentialities, e.g. for love or for music, would it not be rational for him to realize these characteristics rather than make vain attempts to become as rational as possible? There is an enormous variation between different human beings, and this would lead us to modify Aristotle's idea, so that you take more specific rules to be valid for certain individuals with due consideration to their distinctive features. This, in short, is the difference between the ancient Greek idea of self-realization and the modern liberal ideal, expressed for instance by John Stuart Mill, who values individuality very highly. Marx is closer to the traditional Greek opinion.

In some trivial version I believe that this ancient pattern of argument is basic to all arguments about value in Western moral philosophy. When the Greeks asked, what a good life is, they wanted to know which kind of a life suited us. Some were of the same opinion as Aristotle and thought that the answer was "an intellectual life" – the argument is that we are rational animals. The Epicureans instead maintained that pleasure was the only desirable thing – because human beings as a matter of fact strive for pleasure and shun displeasure. In fact this is also the argument of later hedonists: both Bentham and Mill justify hedonism with the proposition that human actions aim as a matter of fact at diminishing displeasure and increasing pleasure. When hedonism is challenged it is usually with the argument that to a human being, it is better to be "a human being dissatisfied than a pig satisfied" (Mill 1863, Chapter II). The Christians believe that human beings are created to meet God and therefore consider the good life to be a blessed contemplation of God. But what does it mean to say that one way of living is better suited to our nature than another?

My version gives the approximate interpretation that the life that suits you is the one you would want to lead when fully informed. This seems not to be too strained an interpretation, and gives a relatively determinate meaning to the phrase. To live as you would really want to when fully informed, can reasonably be taken to suit a vital part of your nature, namely your motivational structure, the central drives and motives of your life. The wants you have when fully informed in some important sense express your nature.[4]

But suppose all human beings (or some group of individuals) have very destructive dispositions? Is the best life for these individuals a very destructive life? If one person devotes his life to hard drinking until he dies from it, another one washes her hands and combs the fringes of her carpets all day, a third one rapes and murders small girls – does not each of them live according to his nature? In a way they do, but these wants must also be opposed to other vital elements of their nature. The wants exemplified are either destructive mainly to the wanter himself, or they are destructive to others (they can of course be both, and most often this

---

[4] This is not the idea defended by Aristotle. But I believe that the concrete recommendations implied by this idea will not be very far from those implied by certain interpretations of an Aristotelian system of morals. The potentialities you have, which ought to be realized to the fullest degree, according to Aristotle, will make you want to dedicate yourself to activities which you are good at and which would make you realize your potentialities. It is probable that Socrates would prefer to continue philosophizing, even though disappointed, rather than live the life of a happy pig. Therefore we believe that the life of the happy pig is not good for Socrates.

is the case). If self-destructive the individual has opposing tendencies: the self-destructive ones tend to undermine his possibilities to go on living and to live a full life in other respects, i.e. his self-destructive tendencies are in conflict with other interests of the same person: to go on living and to be able to do other things he wants. He would be better off, if he was free of his self-destructive tendencies or if someone stopped him from developing and satisfying them. When the individuals concerned are those with destructive tendencies directed mainly against the interests of other persons, these tendencies too in the long run will tend to lash back, since other persons will defend themselves, punish crimes and deeds of violence and so forth. Since all men are dependent on others, it would be for the best of these persons too, if they got rid of their destructive tendencies and fostered other parts of their personality.

Thus I believe that the best interpretation of the ancient idea of living according to one's nature is the one telling you to live the way you would prefer, when fully informed. This idea was sketched in the first chapter of this book and will be spelled out in more detail in Ch. 4. But the problem is how to weigh the interests of different individuals against each other, when they are in conflict. The idea developed in Ch. 5 is that there is a second group of interests, namely the interests in the necessary conditions for satisfaction. I argue that these interests from the moral point of view are more important than the satisfaction of desires. In the sixth chapter a theory of rights is sketched where due consideration is taken of these two kinds of interests.

A central problem in that context is the question whether needs and desires are based in our nature, or are the results of cultural influence. If needs and desires are socially formed throughout, and thus relative to time and type of society, as Marx seems to have maintained, it will be impossible to take them as a starting point for morality. This will be impossible because you have first to answer the question which needs and desires ought to be fostered and satisfied?

Today the issue of the problem of the relativity of needs and desires is further complicated by the fact that the possibility will soon arise of changing human nature by genetic manipulation. As yet this is a theoretical possibility only, but it is a theoretical possibility of great import for moral philosophy of this kind. *If* we can change human nature (and the natures of other creatures, which as a matter of fact is already being done): which changes are desirable? The question of which human needs or desires ought to be changed cannot be answered by reference to the needs and desires we have, or so it seems. Which criteria are then to guide the choice of changes? *Not* changing something when possible is also a choice.

These are difficult problems. I will propose the following tentative solution. First, if we can change a few needs or desires, which are in conflict with the main bulk of the basic needs and genuine desires of someone, e.g. the diabetic's need for extra insulin, or the alcoholic's desire for alcohol, then this is a desirable change, as long as the person himself wants it. Such a change can be evaluated from within a moral system of the type sketched in the preceding chapters. However, to change the nature even of Jack the Ripper against his own will, would be considered bad to himself (provided that he really was well-informed and all things considered didn't want his nature changed, improbable as it may seem) but it *can* in such rare cases be motivated by the needs and desires of others. Thirdly, changing the needs of a human being or an animal very drastically is equal to killing them. Therefore changes of the desires of a person for the sake of others can only be acceptable in those rare cases when his desires are a real threat to the life of other individuals – since one of the main tenets of my moral view is that no one is to be sacrificed merely to increase desire-satisfaction for others. But suppose that you could manipulate the genes of a schizophrenic or a person with Down's syndrome, so that they become "normal": is that to be compared to murder? It doesn't seem so; but on the other hand the personalities of the schizophrenic and the mongoloid will be very radically changed. Here we touch upon problems of personal identity which cannot be solved in this context.

In the long run there might develop the possibility of changing the genes of future generations without changing those who are living now at all, which amounts to determining which species are to live on earth in the future. These types of changes seem more difficult to evaluate according to the standards of the traditional Greek type. It seems as if when changing the nature of living beings you also, in a way, change morality, if morality is relative to the nature of living beings. Thus we can have no criteria for evaluating such replacements of kinds of living beings with other kinds of living beings. I believe that this is true and that if my view of the genesis and validation of ethics is true, then ethics cannot answer such questions. The question "What sort of people should there be?" (the title of a book by Jonathan Glover) has no answer within such a morality. Since this is the only kind of morality that seems to me possible, that question is unanswerable. When we believe that we can answer it, we are in fact considering the question: "In what world do we want to live?" And the answer to that question can only be anchored in our actual interests, rooted in our actual natures.

As you will see in what follows I disregard these complications and try to base a moral theory on needs and desires taken to be given, i.e. neither socially relative, nor changeable except by science fiction methods of genetic manipulation. I do believe however that the theory, when needed, could be developed along the lines indicated here, so that it could be applied to situations where the capacities for genetic manipulation had drastically increased.

Chapter 3

The Modern Discussion of Needs

The concept of 'need' I:
A special kind of desires
It is not uncommon to call a subclass of desires "needs" – exceptionally strong, or congenital desires. Thus the distinction is not made in terms of necessary and sufficient conditions as I will do in Ch. 5. Henry A. Murray, Clark L. Hull, Abraham Maslow, and Herbert Marcuse are among those who use "needs" to refer to a certain class of drives.[1]

A clear example of the use of "need" as a motivational term is to be found in Henry A. Murray:

> A need is a construct (a convenient fiction or hypothetical concept) which stands for a force (the physico-chemical nature of which is unknown) in the brain region, a force which organizes perception, apperception, intellection, conation and action in such a way as to transform in a certain direction an existing, unsatisfying situation. (Murray 1938, 123 f.)

---

[1] Many other psychologists are of the opinion that it is a mistake to use the word "needs" to refer to any kind of drives – needs can give rise to desires, need of water causes thirst for instance – but the drive can never be called a need: see for instance Young 1968, 1. Other psychologists, C.T. Morgan is one, distinguish 'drive' from 'need', but nonetheless recognize a close connection between the two concepts:
"The term *drive* is often used interchangeable with need, but it has the further implication that a need supplies an impetus to behavior. The animal that is hungry or thirsty, for example, appears to be driven in search of food." (Morgan 1956, 57)

I will discuss two different ways to delimit such a class of special desires justifying the name of "needs". The first idea is that you can distinguish true needs from false ones by looking at the origin of the desires: true needs are innate or "natural", while false needs are the result of manipulation or illegitimate external influence (Herbert Marcuse). The second idea is the theory of Abraham Maslow: all normal, human drives are hierarchically ordered in several different levels. It is necessary that the needs of the first level are satisfied, if the needs on the next level are to be actualized, and so forth. It is necessary to satisfy all needs on all levels if an individual is to live a full and rich life. But the needs of the lowest levels are the most basic, and if they are not satisfied for an individual, she will be sick and will not develop the needs of the higher levels. Thus the development of the individual will be stunted.

Innate desires

Marcuse is the clearest example of the first line of reasoning:

> We may distinguish both true and false needs. "False" are those which are superimposed upon the individual by particular social interests in his repression: the needs which perpetuate toil, aggressiveness, misery, and injustice. Their satisfaction might be most gratifying to the individual, but this happiness is not a condition which has to be maintained and protected if it serves to arrest the ability (his own and others) to recognize the disease of the whole and grasp the chances of curing the disease. The result then is euphoria in unhappiness. / - - - /
> No matter how much such needs may have become the individual's own, reproduced and fortified by the conditions of his existence; no matter how much he identifies himself with them and finds himself in their satisfaction, they continue to be what they were from the beginning – products of a society whose dominant interest demands repression. (Marcuse 1964, 4-5)

I suggest that we view the idea of Marcuse as a version of the ancient Greek theme that the best life for a human being is the life in accordance with his original nature. Only our innate desires are genuine expressions of our nature. You may remember that the sixth group of senses of "physis" in the Boas-Lovejoy catalogue was that the natural state is the original one untouched by later changes and degeneration. What is important is not the result of satisfying our desires, but that these desires are really our genuine desires. This of course does not exclude that Marcuse also believes that we will be happiest if we live according to our nature – on the contrary. It is true that Marcuse also maintains that all needs beyond the biological level are socially preconditioned, but he stresses, at least in some texts, that it is not the satisfaction but the causal history that is of importance, when it comes to deciding which desires we ought to satisfy.

A possible interpretation of Marcuse is that he is not strictly interested in our innate desires, but wants to condemn those desires forced upon us by illegitimate methods. In that case the main interest of Marcuse would be our autonomous desires. The 'true needs' of Marcuse would come very close to my 'morally relevant desires' in Ch. 4, although I make the distinction in terms of unchangeability, which I believe put the moral stress where it belongs. And this is not a distinction between 'needs' and 'desires'.

Could the origin and causal history of desires be of moral import? I believe not. There are several problems connected with this idea. First it seems as if it would be very difficult to distinguish the innate desires from those that are socially determined. You could try to look for universal desires, i.e. desires common to human beings from all cultural milieux. But if you make a list of such desires, the list could be both too long and too short. It could include desires, which although not innate, all hitherto known societies have fostered among its members; and there could be genuine needs which would not be counted since they are lacking among people from some culture which has suppressed them.

If you instead tried to study human beings as little touched by cultural influence as possible, you find yourself in a situation similar to Psammetikos, who wanted to know which language was the oldest one, and therefore locked two newborn babies up in the company of dumb nurses in order to hear the first words they spoke on their own.

Even if some of these investigations could be carried through and yielded reliable results, would the results be interesting? Why should needs common to all cultures be more genuine and worthy of satisfaction than those I happen to have? Suppose that we really could know which desires were common to all human beings; it nonetheless seems to me that the diabetic's want of extra insulin has at least an equal claim to satisfaction. And if you knew which needs I would have if not culturally influenced, they do not seem to me more important than those I do have, since cultural influence to a large extent made me the man I am. Untouched by culture I would not be me, indeed I would hardly be human.

The desires of healthy people are needs

Abraham Maslow constructed his famous hierarchy of needs on studies of persons whom he considered psychologically healthy.[2] Desires common to healthy people are genuinely human drives, i.e."needs". The needs are classified into five levels, hierarchically ordered so that the needs at the first level have to be satisfied to a great extent, if the needs at the second level are to develop. Those at the second level must be satisfied before the needs at the third level appear, and so forth. At the first level you find the physiological needs of food, water, oxygen, etc., needs that it is necessary to satisfy if the organism is to survive. At the second level you find needs for security – guarantees that the basic needs will continuously get satisfied. At the third level you find needs of love and belongingness. At the fourth level are needs for self-respect and appreciation from others. At the fifth level there are the needs for self-realization and development. All these needs are according to Maslow quasi-instinctive drives behind human actions; they are universal, as is their relative order; and if they are frustrated, this will result in physical or psychological disturbances.

Later Maslow tried to further refine and develop the fifth level of needs: he distinguished between different needs, either thought to be included among the needs for self-realization or growing up as a sixth level of needs, when self-realization has taken place to a satisfactory degree. Instances of such needs would be needs for knowledge, understanding, beauty, meaning, and symmetry, among others. These are theories I will ignore, since they have not played any great role in the discussions of the theory of Maslow.

I believe that it is not unjust to say that Maslow's theory has not hitherto got much empirical confirmation, if we make an exception for the first two levels.[3] This is first and foremost due to the general lack of clarity and stringency of the theory.

In a way it seems to me that you can take Maslow's theory as a version of a well-known theme in moral philosophy: the concept of the ideal observer as a criterion of good and right, since Maslow maintains

---

[2] A.H. Maslow, "A Theory of Human Motivation", *Psychological Review*, Vol 50, 1943, and *Motivation and Personality*, 1954.

[3] See for example Cofer & Apley, *Motivation: Theory and Research*, 1964, chapter 13. Cf also Fitzgerald, "Abraham Maslow's Hierarchy of Needs – An Exposition and Evaluation", *Human Needs and Politics*, ed. Fitzgerald 1977.

that his empirical studies yield normative results.[4] But Maslow's version is marred by some weaknesses. The first is why are the universal human needs most important? Why not pay the same attention to more individual needs? If a man is very different from the "healthy man" of Maslow, should we disregard his needs? Maslow might object that all human beings in fact have the same needs. But this is not in accordance with what Maslow himself says, namely that the needs appear in their true form only among healthy persons. If a man gets his needs satisfied from the beginning, he will be healthy and develop the needs in due order. But if this is not the case – should we not satisfy the needs of the sick man? Some have innate illnesses which give rise to special needs. It seems to me that the needs of the sick would be of particular moral urgency.

Secondly, "the healthy human being", the criterion of Maslovian needs is clearly a normative concept although Maslow maintains the opposite.[5] The individuals Maslow has chosen to study in order to construct his hierarchy of needs, are partly great spirits from history (Spinoza and Einstein among others – not Marx and Strindberg!) partly students and friends of Maslow. The criteria of selection are never clearly stated, but I suspect that there is a kind of circle built into the selection: healthy are those who have the needs of Maslow, and *vice versa*. Anyhow, they are described by Maslow as some species of American middle-class heroes: they are all very intelligent, successful, not very radical and have a condescending attitude towards their less prosperous fellow beings.

Thirdly: we might perhaps suppose that even the heroes of Maslow

---

[4] "If it is objected by the technical philosopher, 'How can you prove that it is better to be happy than unhappy?' even this question can be answered empirically, for if we observe human beings under sufficiently wide conditions we discover that they, *they* themselves, *not* the observer choose spontaneously to be happy rather than unhappy, comfortable rather than pained, serene rather than anxious." (Maslow 1970, 272.)
Cf also: "It /Maslow's concept of normality/ implies a strictly naturalistic system of values that can be enlarged by further empirical research with human nature. Such research should be able to give us answers to the age-old questions 'How can I be a good man?' 'How can I live a good life?'" (Maslow 1970, 279)

[5] "Being a desire of healthy individuals" is not the only condition to be reckoned a human need. Maslow also requires that frustration leads to illness: "The chronic lack of the satisfier produces pathology." (Maslow 1971, 382) But I want to concentrate on the first condition.

sometimes want to suppress their fellows, rape someone, or murder a competitor. Such desires cannot reasonably be included among the human desires which ought to be satisfied according to Maslow. So we must also have a criterion to decide which of the desires of these ideal persons do belong, and which do not, to the class of needs. Maybe it is here that the idea of harmful effects of frustration comes in as a further criterion, or they do not qualify since not common to all?

Anyhow it seems clear that Maslow needs evaluations to be able to judge whether or not there is a need, and whether or not it ought to be satisfied – although Maslow himself denies all this.

I do not deny that we have the needs postulated by Maslow's theory, but neither do I believe that it is confirmed beyond doubt that we have them. I will not deny that it would be of great interest especially when we are pondering questions of welfare politics, if Maslow's theory could be proved true. But I cannot see that Maslovian needs have a greater claim to be satisfied than well-informed desires of the kind I will delimit in Ch. 4. Furthermore I believe that needs defined as in Ch. 5 – as necessary and sufficient means to desired ends – are of greater moral import than are Maslow's needs.[6]

---

[6] There are other ways of distinguishing between 'true' and 'false' needs', e.g. the attempts by Karen Horney and Simone Weil to distinguish between 'true needs' and 'neurotic needs'. Karen Horney and Simone Weil take the possibility of satisfaction to be the defining criterion of true needs: irrespective of how much you try to satisfy a neurotic need, the person having it will feel dissatisfied. But when it comes to genuine needs, this is not the case. See e.g."Das neurotische Liebesbedürfnis" *Zentralblatt für Psychotherapie,* 10, 1937.

Simone Weil expresses a similar idea in the following words: "Le premier caractere qui distingue les besoins des désirs des fantaisies ou des vices, et les nourritures des gourmandises ou des poisons, c'est que les besoins sont limités, ainsi que les nourritures qui leur correspondent. Un avare n'a jamais assez d'or, mais pour tot homme, si on lui donne du pain a discretion, il viendra un moment ou il en aura assez. La nourriture apporte le rassasiement." (Weil 1952, 16-17)

It is true that unsatisfiable desires seem normatively impotent; we can have no obligation to satisfy them, if 'ought' implies 'can'. But this distinction does not seem to draw a line between more and less important interests, since many trivial desires seem easy to satisfy, e.g. my desire to have an ice-cream, to listen to some music, look at tv, etc., while others are at least as important although very difficult or impossible to satisfy, e.g. my want to be saved from dying from cancer, or to get my physical mobility back after a stroke.

The concept of 'needs' II:
Necessary conditions

Quite a different way of analysing 'need' is to take it not as a subclass of desires but as connected with necessary conditions for desired goals. The English word "need" can be used both as a noun and as a modal verb: roughly with the same meaning as "must" or "it is necessary that". In German and French the corresponding words, "Bedürfnis" and "besoin" respectively, do not lend themselves to be used as verbs, but the interpretation of constructions with these words in many contexts can be analysed in terms of necessary conditions for some goal. The same seems to be true also of some non-European languages, which I have tried to check with the help of friends of mine.[7] In the Persian language there are two different expressions roughly equivalent to "need": "niaz" and "ehtiaj" (transcribed to the Latin alphabet). Both are constructed with the Persian equivalent to the verb "to have", "dashtan": "niaz dashtan" a little more ceremoniously, and "ehtiaj dashtan" which is more colloquial. From the word "niaz" also can be constructed the adjective and the substantival "niazmand", referring to the miserable ones, those who lack the necessities of life. In Turkish you also find two words which can be connected with "need", "ihtiyac" and "gerek". The former word indicates "being in need", "suffer misery", "being poor". The adjective "gerek" means "necessary" but also "fit" and "proper".

In Utta Kim Wawrzinek's article on "Bedürfnis" in *Geschichtliche Grundbegriffe* (ed. Brunner, Conze, & Koselleck, 1972) the German "Bedürfniss" is analysed in three components:
1. Necessity – unless your needs are satisfied, you will suffer harm.
2. Legitimacy – needs give rise to legitimate claims.
3. Psychological drive – needs influences behaviour.

The third element I have already discussed and dismissed. Therefore I will concentrate on the first two elements. I will first discuss what others have had to say on the first condition: what does it mean to say that needs must be satisfied to avoid harm?

Several authors have thought that you ought to distinguish between two concepts of 'need': one referring to necessary conditions for any goal and another referring to the necessary conditions for a minimally acceptable life, or something like that. Kai Nielsen (1963 and 1969), Georg Henrik von Wright (1982), David Wiggins (1985), David

---

[7] Ali Kassiri helped me with the notes on the Persian language, which would be typical of middle class use of language in Teheran in the end of the 1970s. Hüseiyin Saracer gave me the information on Turkish.

Braybrooke (1987), and Garrett Thomson (1987) all agree that you ought to distinguish between "needs" in an instrumental and "needs" in a categorical or absolute sense. In the latter case the goal can be left out without the resulting phrase being elliptical, and in this case only you can talk about needs in a strong sense. (Cf Ch. 5.) All agree further that the individual who does not get her needs satisfied, suffers harm. But how is 'harm' to be analysed?

Wiggins writes:

> What constitutes suffering or wretchedness or harm is an essentially contestable matter, and it is to some extent relative to a culture, even to some extent relative to people's conceptions of suffering, wretchedness and harm. Obviously there is much more to be said about that (even if it is doubtful how much of it involves the idea of 'relative deprivation' – a relativity we have ventured to omit altogether from the argument); but instead let us hurry on... (Wiggins 1985, 155)

This is rather typical: most authors take harm to be relative to evaluations, conventions, social circumstances, and so forth. But this makes the concept less useful for social critique and moral theory, because needs then will be relative.

Knut Erik Tranøy takes another line in an article from 1972-75 on 'needs'. He there distinguishes between 'vital needs' and 'legitimate needs', which harks back to his doctoral dissertation *On the Logic of Normative Systems* from 1953. There he distinguished between two kinds of goals: "prerequisite goals" and "fulfilment goals". The difference was explained in the following way:

> A set of goals (x) will be said to be prerequisite to the attainment of another goal or set of goals (y) if attainment of all of the former goals (x) is a necessary but insufficient condition for attainment of (y) (the fulfilment goals). This definition entails that non-attainment of one of the goals in x is a sufficient condition for non-attainment of all of the goals in y. (Tranøy 1953, 172)

That the distinction between 'vital needs' and 'legitimate needs' is related to that between 'prerequisite' and 'fulfilment goals' is indicated by Tranøy himself in a footnote in 1975 (162). I believe that Tranøy is on the right track here: needs must be satisfied if we are to be able to satisfy our desires. However, I believe that we must be more explicit when it comes to stating what is necessary for any satisfactory life in order to get a clear grasp of what is involved in the concept of 'needs'. This I have tried to do in Ch. 5. Other authors have tried to use some concept of a "normal human life" to delimit the class of basic needs. David Braybrooke for instance makes a list of "course-of-life-needs", which all would agree must be satisfied if we are to be able to function "without derangement in carrying out the tasks assigned a person in a certain combination of basic social roles" (Braybrooke 1987, 47). For every need there is a minimum level of satisfaction – but where this level is, is not stated by Braybrooke. He presupposes that most of us fulfil (or would want to fulfil?) the roles as "parent, householder, worker, and citizen" (Braybrooke 1987, 48). The list seems rather arbitrary. Many lack one or more of these roles: do they still have the needs connected with the role they lack, or do they lack some needs? To many the role of lover is the the most essential in life. Let us suppose that this is true of Quasimodo, the crippled bell-ringer of Notre Dame – do any obligations arise from his erotic needs? You do not get any answer to such questions from Braybrooke.

The problem with Braybrooke is that he presupposes a normal middle-class life in a Western industrialized country. Let us instead for a moment consider a male indian in the North American plains in the beginning of the 19th century, an enlightened Boddhisattva in India or Kristina of Stommeln (a medieval saint described by a Swedish monk, Peter of Dacia). Their lives differ radically from each other and from the man Braybrooke has in mind: who lives the most normal human life? I believe that their needs will differ too. Suppose for instance that we want to know which needs must be satisfied during childhood. The answer will depend on who the child will be as grown up.

David Miller (1976) makes needs relative to the plan of life of the person concerned: what is necessary to carry this plan through is what the person needs. But it is not improbable that we choose plan of life partly as a result of which needs were satisfied and which frustrated while we were children. So we seem to move in a circle: to have that plan of life, you have to get those needs satisfied. And as I have pointed out elsewhere (pp 47f, 55f, and 105ff), many things can be central to my plan of life, which cannot reasonably be called needs.

Some modern philosophers try to revive the Aristotelian concept of "human nature", when discussing the concept of 'need', among them Elisabeth Anscombe (1958) and H.J. McCloskey (1976). The reason is of course that an analysis of 'need' in terms of necessary conditions, implies some goal, and the function of man could be such a goal. McCloskey even maintains that the concept of 'need' cannot be given a clear meaning outside an Aristotelian system. On the other hand in Aristotle's own texts the concept of 'need' does not play a central part. Even if we do not accept the idea of a function of man, we might want to relate the concept of 'need' to some idea of the normal functioning of man. Braybrooke's analysis in terms of normal social roles might be taken to be an instance. But there are difficulties – what is normal? If we start out with the body, is it the body of Carl Lewis that is normal, or is it mine? It does not seem reasonable to take some statistical average to be the norm of normality either, since we will then have to decide which group is the relevant one for comparisons, is the relevant group the entire population of the earth just now? Then the statistical average will reckon certain levels of malnutrition and diseases as normal. Is it white males in the Western industrialized society? If so a certain excess of weight will be normal. Consequently the needs would be relative to the comparison group. But to take the healthy and happy individual as the normal one – however unusual this fortunate creature is – involves other difficulties. If we take the good life to be the normal life, I think that our concept of 'need' will be too inclusive.

Georg Henrik von Wright however is an author who seems to take this line of thought. In an article published in Swedish in 1982 von Wright distinguishes between elliptical statements of needs, those that state that something is necessary in order to reach some arbitrary goal, and non-elliptical statements of needs, those that concern what is necessary in order to live well. The non-elliptical use can be formulated thus: "A creature *needs*, what it is *bad* for it to lack." (von Wright 1982, 1; all translations from this article by RO.) If the goal presupposed by a need-statement is human welfare, then the statement is not elliptical even if the goal is not mentioned. The reason is that welfare is not a contingent goal for a human being. It is not chosen in the same way that for instance someone can choose to become a good football player. The latter is a goal for some people but not for others. Those who want to become good at football need more training than others do. But such a statement about a need must mention the goal or else the statement is elliptical. Welfare is not a contingent goal, and therefore we can say that we need what is necessary for our welfare without mentioning the goal: it is so to say implied by the concept of a 'need' itself. 'Needs' are tied, as far as human beings are concerned, to the concept of 'welfare', which is not to be analysed in material terms, but in terms of the feelings of people. It is not necessary, however, that people always know their true needs. Indeed, they are not always aware of whether they are faring well or not.

'Welfare' / 'misfortune' are according to von Wright "physiognomic concepts", which means that it is empirically observable whether a person fares well or not. He compares with the flourishing and languishing of a plant, which are both observable. I believe that von Wright tries to bridge the gap between 'is' and 'ought' with these physiognomic concepts. The Humean will not be convinced of course: either welfare is observable and it is an open question whether welfare ought to be striven for, or it is something desirable and observable, but its desirability is not observable. But how are we to draw the line between "flourishing" and "languishing"?

"What a human being needs for his welfare or not to fare ill, could also be called what a human being needs *qua human being*." (von Wright 1982, 10)

It seems as if von Wright considers welfare to be the natural state. In connection with 'health' / 'illness', he says: "Health is the natural state of a creature." (von Wright 1982, 9) The welfare of man consists partly of health, partly of happiness. If happiness according to von Wright is also the natural state of human beings is not clearly stated. Where to draw the border between illness and health can perhaps be determined by medical science, although the limit must be somewhat vague. More unclear, however, is where to draw the line between happiness and unhappiness. Unhappiness can be observed according to von Wright:

/Unhappiness/ shows itself, partly in the evaluation of her life situation by the human being herself, partly in her actual way of living. Different forms of aggressive and asocial behaviour, flight from responsibility, ruthlessness, and meanness towards others, insensitivity and selfishness can be objective signs, showing that a human being is not well off, irrespective of how she herself "feels". (von Wright 1982, 10)

von Wright does not penetrate the question of where to draw the limit between welfare and misery, he seems to presuppose that they are dichotomies – either we fare well or we fare ill. I believe, however, that if we put stress in this way on 'faring well', there will be no definite difference between elliptical and non-elliptical uses of 'needs', since there must be several contingent goals we must reach in order really to thrive. The man who is forced by circumstances to give up a career as opera singer to provide for his family as a school teacher, is harmed in a way in not living as well as he could – the example is mine, not von Wright's. But it does not seem reasonable to say that he has a basic need for the economic resources that would make possible his career as an opera singer. The boundary between serious harm and an acceptable life must be put lower.[8] Where to draw the line seems to be arbitrary. The capacity for development varies from individual to individual. The space for development is furthermore dependent upon the economic and social level of different societies. And most of us have capacities for developments which cannot be realized conjointly: if I am to be a good singer I will have to forego the developing of my pedagogic skills and *vice versa*.

If instead we lay stress upon not faring ill, I believe that we move in the right direction towards a definition of "need" in terms of a minimally acceptable level of human existence. But we do not get much help from von Wright in characterizing such a level, except the notion that it should include health. Should we then take the relevant concept to be full health according to the criteria of WHO or just to mean the absence of life-threatening illnesses?

But von Wright himself seems most prone to count everything necessary to our well-being as needs. We can be *mistaken* about these conditions – then we develop *false needs*. However, he indicates that we do not need to get all our desires satisfied to live well. But too great a discrepancy between desires and satisfaction is harmful (von Wright 1982, 7). Furthermore von Wright is of the opinion that we also need what is necessary to fulfil our duties. But that question will be discussed in the last part of this section.

Let us summarize: a concept of 'need' based on 'welfare', 'thriving', 'to live a good life' or something like that seems to me to be too inclusive – it does not help us to distinguish between urgent and less urgent interests. A better way seems to be to define "basic needs" in terms of a minimally acceptable life, but this is not spelled out by von Wright.

The best analysis of 'basic needs' hitherto in my view is that of Garrett Thomson, who analyses 'need' in terms of 'harm', which in turn is analysed in terms of 'interests'. Thomson's idea of 'interest' is as far as I know an invention of his own. He maintains that we have by nature certain interests, which it is not possible to change; therefore certain of our goals are given. Unless there are unchangeable interests, needs will be relative; we would have needs under the condition that we had chosen certain goals but not in other cases. But we cannot choose or change our interests. I believe that this theory is naturalistic in a way, and I find it interesting. Thomson tries to take a middle path between a theory stating that something is good for someone because desired by

---

[8] Cf Walsh 1961, who is of a different opinion: he maintains that every impediment to our potentialities is an evil.

her, and an objectivistic theory stating that something is good iff desirable. The middle path is a detour through a theory of interests, which are taken to be "the reasons which lie behind a person's non-instrumental desires". (Thomson 1987, 64) The ontological status of interests is never clearly explained by Thomson, but he tells us that the interests need not be conscious, they are not the agent's own (conscious) reasons for desires, but they are what explain the desires. Interests are not chosen. They are general, not particular. They are some kind of basic and unconscious elements of our motivational set-up. If they are satisfied, this is good for us, if they are frustrated this is bad for us. Thomson distinguishes between "secondary" and "primary goods" instead of "instrumental" and "intrinsic values", since the terms "extrinsic" and "intrinsic" can, he claims, be confusing: harm means by definition something bad, and therefore it could be reasonable to call harm intrinsically bad. However harm is only secondarily bad, since it is bad because it deprives us of something primarily good, i.e. satisfaction of our interests.

The usual way to interpret "interests" is to take them to be some kind of objective desires – they are the desires someone *ought* to have or *would* have if fully informed.[9] But this is not Thomson's idea. He takes interests to be an underlying structure of abstract desires, which a person has without being aware of them, abstract desires which give rise to and explain his concrete and specific desires. We can for instance have interests in status and love, but not in being appreciated by the Nobel-committee and loved by Madonna. Desires – even the rational and well-informed ones – are particular, while the interests are general and abstract. Desires involve choices or hypothetical choices – which is not true of the interests: the latter are presuppositions of choices although not the conscious reasons for them. As far as I understand Thomson, the interests are nonetheless specific to each person, although many of them can be common, even common to all human beings. It furthermore seems, although Thomson is not quite clear at this point, that the interests are what *make* certain states primarily good, not the other way round, that we are interested in those things that as a matter of fact *are* good. When our interests are satisfied we feel satisfaction, but we might not always feel satisfied when our desires are satisfied, which is

---

[9] Cf Hare 1963, 122: "To have an interest is, crudely speaking, for there to be something which one wants, or is likely in the future to want, or which is (or is likely to be) a means necessary or sufficient for the attainment of something which one wants (or is likely to want)."

explained by the fact that we can be mistaken about our real interests. But it is not the experienced satisfaction that makes these states desirable, they are desirable since they are the goals of our interests. The interests are anchored in our nature and therefore we cannot choose our primary values arbitrarily. What can have value for us is conditioned by our nature. If no desires were anchored in our nature, we could ask whether they ought to be satisfied or if it would be better to change them. But if there are interests which cannot be changed, then we have got an Archimedean point of ethics. Although I do not accept Thomson's analysis of 'interests'. I agree that interests – but in a more traditional sense meaning well-informed desires that we cannot change – in a way constitute the ground of morality.

According to Garrett Thomson we need what is necessary to avoid harm; and we are harmed iff we are prevented from satisfying our interests.(Thomson 1987, 76.) No clearer account of 'harm' is given. Primarily Thomson takes harm to be lack of primary valuable states. But he acknowledges that "/h/arm can and often does involve intrinsically undesirable states of mind, like feeling miserable and being in pain." (Thomson 1987, 37) This notwithstanding Thomson is of the opinion that primary bad states of consciousness are bad because they prevent us from positively valuable activities or from appreciating them. The idea of harm as a privation furthermore explains that persons can be harmed without noticing it. Thus death can be a serious harm, even though no one experiences it.

Since Thomson analyses 'harm' in terms of loss and lack, his analysis can be taken to go along with that of von Wright. But this is not the whole truth:

> Need is tied to the absence of certain primary goods rather than to their loss, and so, to characterize 'need' in terms of 'harm', should explain harm in the following way: a person is harmed whenever this level of well-being is below a certain level or norm, even if it has not actually fallen. (Thomson 1987, 93)

"Harm" – as it is to be interpreted in statements of needs – means that you are below a certain level or norm unless the needs are satisfied. But we get no information on the position of this level. "It is not fixed how well a person's interests have to be met for him to attain the norm of well-being, to be or fall below which constitutes harm." (*Ibid.*)

The boundary between harm and non-harm is vague, but this is of no importance according to Thomson, as long as we can agree upon the degree of urgency of different needs. In that case we need not know

exactly the boundary between "urgent" and "non-urgent".
Thomson introduces experienced suffering as a criterion of insufficient satisfaction of needs: "...harm and need typically involve bad and disliked states of mind. To this extent, the distinction between harm and benefit is one of kind rather than degree." (Thomson 1987, 94) But it is not clear how great weight Thomson puts on negative mental states, since he is anxious to give an analysis of 'primary value' which is not conceived exclusively in terms of desirable/undesirable mental states. Anyhow, I do not believe that a criterion formulated in terms of disliked mental states is a good one. There are pain-sensations and other disliked feelings which nonetheless are not serious enough to be characterized as *harm*: the feeling of exhaustion in the last few hundred metres of a 10,000 metres run, the itching in your scalp when you have got lice.

I believe that in the great outlines an analysis of basic needs in terms of harm is on the right track, but that to be useful in normative contexts, it ought to be made more precise by defining some minimal level of well-being. In Ch. 5 I will make an attempt to draw the line a little more precisely.

Further conditions

As you may remember from the above-mentioned article in *Geschichtliche Grundbegriffe*, it is often felt that needs give rise to legitimate claims. Some authors go so far as to maintain that the concept of 'need' is basically a normative concept, e.g. R.S. Peters (1958), Anthony Flew (1977), and Kate Soper (1981). To say that someone needs something is to say that she ought to get it according to this view. Kai Nielsen does not go so far, but he maintains that a statement that someone has a need for something pragmatically implies the statement that he ought to get it. Many authors have tried to formulate further conditions to make sure that need-claims really are legitimate.

Knut Erik Tranøy proposes in his article on needs (Tranøy 1975) that if a person, a, has a need, then the satisfaction of of it, "does not necessarily (essentially) block any of the vital, or all of the non-vital, legitimate needs of b (where a may or may not be identical with b)" (Tranøy 1975, 155). It must also be the case that the satisfaction of a need of a "does not necessarily hurt b (again it may or may not be the case that $a=b$)". (*Ibid.*) Another author who has a similar restriction is David Miller (1976):

...I suggest, when we interpret justice as the equal satisfaction of needs, we should discount those needs which (necessarily, not merely contingently) cannot be satisfied consistently with their equal satisfaction on the part of others. (Miller 1976, 141)

I am not quite sure what "necessarily" means in these contexts and what importance Trangøy or Miller ascribe it. Are the needs of the sadist of the kind that they *necessarily* block the satisfaction of the needs of others, or does the satisfaction of sadistic needs *necessarily* hurt others? Maybe – unless the sadist is satisfied by making masochists suffer. But let us consider a different case: suppose a man has a bad heart. The only heart that would suit him and save his life is the heart of his brother, who of course needs his own heart. If the surgeons – heaven forbids – took the heart of the brother and saved him, would the satisfaction of the sick man's need block the satisfaction of his brother's needs "necessarily" or only as a contingent matter of fact? If it blocks it necessarily, can the same be said of the brother – so that we cannot say that he needs his own heart?

This distinction seems not to be of moral importance to me. It is possible to say that the sick man has a need for the heart of his brother, but that this need is in conflict with the needs of his brother. Whether we should satisfy a desire or not cannot be decided before we have taken into consideration possible conflicts between the desire and possible needs. The same seems to be true of needs. Even the most "innocent" needs can come into conflict in certain circumstances. It is difficult to see why certain kinds of needs would be disqualified *a priori*, so that they are not even considered, when different needs are weighted against each other. If we try to build such a restriction into the definition of "need", we will be forced to decide which conflicts between needs are such as to disqualify the claims for need-satisfaction in those situations before we can even say that someone has a need. This seems to me odd.

Other authors build in moral restrictions in different ways. Some state that the goal, presupposed by a need-statement, is to meet certain moral requirements. von Wright for instance counts necessary means for complying with our obligations as needs. It is not impossible to say that I need a certain sum of money in order to pay my debts. But I will not count it as a basic need. It could be argued that since moral requirements are unconditional (at least if Kant is right) it is a basic need of everyone to have the necessary means to fulfil their obligations. Plant, Lesser, & Taylor-Gooby (1980) argue that we need freedom, because every moral statement to the effect that someone ought to do something implies that the agent is free to perform his duty ('ought' implies 'can'). Therefore other persons ought not to restrict our freedom in an arbitrary way.

However, I suggest that the needs connected with our ability to perform morally right actions are instrumental needs relative to the goal of being morally good. "If you want to be an honest person, you need give back the money that you borrowed." But I want not to include the necessary means to a morally good life, among the basic needs, since I want to base morals on a non-moral account of needs in the way sketched in Ch. 1, 5 and 6. I thus take it that basic needs should be defined solely in terms of harm, analysed as I do in Ch. 5.

David Wiggins also introduces some moral considerations in his definition of "need", although in a characteristically obscure way:

> Where needing is concerned, however, the definition of alternativeness must it seems be modified to restrict the class of alternative futures $\geq t$ that (i) are economically or technologically conceivable and (ii) do not involve us in morally (or otherwise) unacceptable acts ... (Wiggins 1985, 156; also to be found in Wiggins 1987.)

Either the idea is that a person has needs of everything necessary to realize the economically, technically, and morally possible future state, in which we avoid getting harmed, or the idea is that we sometimes can have a need *even though* the satisfaction of it will involve us in immoral acts – namely if this is the only possible way to avoid harm. The moral proviso in (ii) then would have the purpose of acknowledging that we *can* have a categorical need even in those situations where satisfaction of this need is not strictly logically or physically necessary, but only so to say *morally necessary*. This latter interpretation seems to me possible, although a bit strained.

In any case I do not want moral considerations smuggled into the definition of 'need'. That is I do not want to define 'need' in such a way that you have to make a normative decision when you are to decide whether an individual has a need or not. I suggest that if P in the situation *s* has several possible ways to avoid getting below the minimally acceptable level, but where some of the ways involve immoral acts, then P in *s* has a need for the disjunction of the means necessary for the goal. If only one of the ways does not involve immoral acts, then P has a need for the means to realize that possible state in order to live an acceptable *and* moral life.

Needs and justice

Nowhere else in normative discourse has the concept of 'needs' so often been used as in discussions of justice. Since the first Christians distributed their resources "to each according to his needs", the idea has been proclaimed again and again that justice basically consists in satisfying the most fundamental needs of everyone. The socialist slogan "to each according to his needs, from each according to his capacity" was touched upon in Ch. 2. Now I want to discuss this slogan a little more in detail.

Brian Barry (1965 and 1973) is of the opinion that needs never can play a central role in a political discussion concerning ultimate political principles of distribution, since in such discussions the *goals* are what matter, and needs are just means to goals. *Given* certain goals the needs will be important, but in ultimate principles they do not matter. My opinion is the opposite: basic needs are what matter in political and moral theory, while the more abstract theories of intrinsic value are rather unimportant. Rawls' idea that justice concerns the distribution of primary goods is a related conception.

Many authors have been of the opinion that need-satisfaction is important from the viewpoint of justice. David Miller and James Sterba are two philosophers who make this connection. It is true that David Miller (1976) does not take the principle "to each according to his needs" to be the only ultimate principle of justice. He distinguishes between three different principles of justice, which he believes grow out of different social circumstances. The most general formulation Miller gives to the principle of justice is "to each his due" (Miller 1976, 20). This is, according to Miller, the formal theory of justice, which must be specified by stating what counts as each one's due.

According to Miller there are three main candidates for the role of substantial principle of justice. The first one says that what is due to someone is what is hers according to law and tradition – a representative of this theory is David Hume. David Miller identifies such theories with theories of rights. I find this identification unreasonable, since you can formulate theories of rights which do not take established rights for granted, but which state principles of rights which we *ought* to respect, whether or not they are established by society. Theories of rights are connected by Miller with the feudal society, although such theories were first and foremost formulated during the transition from feudalism to capitalism.

The second idea of justice says that the due share of the resources of society is proportionate to one's merit or contribution. This is a theory which Miller connects with the capitalist market society, although the idea emanates from Aristotle (*Nicomachean Ethics* book V). Lastly we have the idea that the resources of society are to be distributed according to needs, a principle which Miller maintains is first and foremost valid in small groups kept together by emotional ties of solidarity and love, e.g. groups with family relations or based on common ideology or religion. I believe on the contrary that no family can use the principle of needs or else some member of the family will feel wronged. In the family, if anywhere, you have to follow a strict and mechanical model of equality or a rigorous system of merit, just because of the emotional ties and the import of how one is treated on one's self-esteem. It is much easier to be generous and recognize the claims of needs of a stranger than of your brother.

Miller's opinion is that our modern conception of justice contains elements from all three ideas. But I want to discuss just his idea of what the third principle amounts to. Miller analyses the concept of 'need' in the following way: "'A needs X' = 'A will suffer harm if he lacks X'." (Miller 1976, 130) So far his analysis is on the same lines as the analysis in Ch. 5. What counts as "harm" according to Miller is determined by a person's "plan of life": "... to determine what counts as harm for any given person, it is necessary first to identify the aims and activities which are central to that person's way of life." (Miller 1976, 132f)

> Harm, for any given individual, is whatever interferes directly or indirectly with the activities essential to his plan of life; and correspondingly, his needs must be understood to comprise whatever is necessary to allow these activities to be carried out. (Miller 1976, 134)

Then comes the addition that the plan of life of a person must be "intelligible to us /.../ in the sense that we can understand how, for the person who has it, that plan of life has significance and value" (Miller 1976, 135): we do not say of a pyromaniac that he needs matches but that he needs psychiatric treatment. Moreover we must not count as needs such needs which necessarily cannot be satisfied to the same degree for all. An example is the need of *higher* status than others (Miller 1976, 141). You do not get to know what Miller thinks of needs which do not necessarily block the satisfaction of others to the same degree, but which presuppose the cooperation of others if they are to be satisfied, such as sexual needs. If love is essential to my plan of life – what conclusions are we to draw from Miller's theory of justice?

I have already touched *en passant* upon problems connected with defining "needs" in relation to lifeplans and the problems connected with requiring compatibility between needs. But let us disregard them for the moment. Now the principle of justice says that a just distribution is one that satisfies the basic needs of as many as possible of those concerned. I will mention two problems for such a principle: what are we to do if all basic needs can not be met conjointly? And what principle is valid for the distribution of the surplus – if there is any – which remains when all basic needs are satisfied?

The first problem is not discussed by Miller, as far as I have seen. The latter problem, however, is discussed by him, although his solution is not satisfactory, as I will try to show. Miller introduces a scale of well-being for every individual, constructed in the following way:

> ... each person is asked to consider all the possible ways in which resources might be allocated to him, over and above the allocation which satisfies his needs. He is also asked to indicate which allocation he would regard as giving him the greatest well-being, and which he would regard as giving him the least; and then to place other allocations on a scale between these two extreme points... We can interpret the principle of equal well-being as the claim that each man should enjoy as high a position on his scale as every other. (Miller 1976, 144)

Such a scale presupposes that the desires of each individual are limited; if the scale is infinite, every point on it will be as far from the endpoint as every other. Therefore we must presuppose that the desires are limited; otherwise Miller's scale will not work.

Miller requires that we should satisfy an equal proportion of each person's desires, i.e. that each person is to come proportionally as high on his scale of well-being, as is compatible with everyone else's reaching proportionally as high on hers. (Miller 1976, 144) But why require proportionate equality – why not simple equality? Miller's idea is akin to William Frankena's idea of justice presented in "Some Beliefs about Justice" (1966).[10] If a person has a greater potential for

---

[10] The idea is already present in Frankena 1963, 41, but with the important amendment that the principle of proportional satisfaction is to be used when a certain level of well-being for all is reached. This idea may be hinted at also in his "Some Beliefs about Justice" on p 15: "I am somewhat inclined to agree that society should try to make available to everyone the same general level of material possessions, at least up to a certain point." Thus my accusation against Frankena might be unjust.(!)

satisfaction, he can get much more satisfaction than another even when the other has reached his maximum satisfaction. Let us assume that we are considering the question of how to use a sum of money – the last sum left in the treasury of the borough, and let us assume that the sum cannot be divided. Either we can give an artist a stipend or we can give a handicapped person more travel vouchers. According to Frankena and Miller it can be just to give the money to the artist, *even if* the artist has a much better life than the handicapped person, and the life of the latter would be much better if he got the money, although less good than the artist's would be without the money, *provided* that the artist has a potentiality for greater satisfaction. The reason then would be that he is further from his maximum than is the handicapped person. To me it seems as if the reason in favour of giving the money to the handicapped person is much stronger – he is much worse off.

There are two possible defenses of the standpoint of Frankena and Miller. Either you assume that unsatisfied desires are painful, or you take every maximally satisfying life (i.e. every life where someone realizes his maximal satisfaction) to be of exactly the same value. In either case you get a reason to give the stipend to the artist rather than travel vouchers to the handicapped person. But are the assumptions reasonable? Suppose that the artist has five desires unsatisfied: to get the stipend, to go to Paris, to sell a picture to the National Museum of Arts, to get the opportunity to decorate a tube-station, and that his best friend becomes a critic on a prestigious art journal. The handicapped has just two desires which are not satisfied: to be able to sleep without pain in the night, and to be able to go and see his friend more often. You cannot satisfy one of the handicapped person's desires, until the artist has got at least two or three of his desires satisfied. This does not seem morally compelling.

The other possibility is somewhat more plausible. If the artist and the handicapped person have got exactly half of their desires satisfied, their lives are equally valuable. This differs a little from the consequence of traditional hedonism – that the lives of different persons are of unequal value simply because one of them is happier than than the other. There is something appalling in the idea that if you can only save one life, you ought to choose the one with the greatest prospects of being happy. But this might be a consequence even of the idea that the value of life depends on how many desires are satisfied: the one with the best prospects of becoming satisfied is to be saved, if this idea is combined with utilitarianism. There is however a kind of equality built into the idea that two persons with all their desires satisfied have equally good lives. But both Frankena and Miller seem to presuppose that this is not the case, they seem to presuppose that some people have greater capacity for being satisfied (or in the case of Frankena to be happy). This also seems to be the view of common sense: some people have more and more easily satisfiable desires than others. Why not accept that they have better lives than the rest? If so, it seems to me that the idea of proportionate satisfaction ought to be rejected; the fact that someone has a greater capacity for satisfaction is not a reason for giving him more satisfaction than the one with the lesser capacity.

It is common among socialists to maintain that justice consists in a distribution according to needs and desires. So I want to examine this idea a little more.

A first version of the socialist idea is often ascribed to Marx: a distribution is just when all desires are satisfied.[11]

... /die Kommunisten/ erstreben nur eine solche Organisation der Produktion und des Verkehrs die ihnen die normale, d.h.nur durch die Bedürfnisse selbst beschränkte, Befriedigung aller Bedürfnisse möglich macht. (Marx 1845-46, Marx-Engels, *Werke*, Bd 3, 239 note)

That Marx is to be interpreted in this way is maintained by Cornelius Castoriadis (1984) and Patricia Springborg (1981). As Castoriadis points out, Marx' idea of material affluence presupposes that the needs and desires are delimited, while in other places he denies this. Furthermore it seems as if we had no need for a theory of justice, if it were possible to satisfy all desires conjointly. Justice is necessitated by the scarcity of resources, as has been maintained at least since Hume.

---

[11] It seems possible to ascribe such a theory also to Gerrard Winstanley and William Morris. They are not very clear, but they describe distribution in their utopias in a way that makes such an interpretation plausible. Winstanly for instance says that goods are to be gathered in common stores, where "... every Family may fetch what they want for food or pleasure." (*The Law of Freedom. The Works of Gerrard Winstanley*, ed. Sabine, New York 1941, quoted from the second edition 1965, 583). On the other hand Winstanly also hints that the laws and the civil servants are to "...regulate the unrational practice of such men..." /viz covetous, proud, and beastly-minded men," who want more than others or waste common goods/. In William Morris' future ideal society described in *News from Nowhere*, the *alter ego* of the author wanting a pipe, goes into a "shop", chooses a beautifully worked pipe, mounted in gold sprinkled with little gems, but he does not pay anything. (See chapter VI, p 217 in *Three Works by William Morris*, London 1977.)

(Hume 1777, Section III) So this interpretation gives us no guidance in questions of distribution of the type we are normally considering. So let us try some other interpretations! I can think of three more interpretations, but none of them seems to me more acceptable. Let's first try this interpretation: "Satisfy all basic needs of all members of the society, and distribute the surplus – if there is any – so that every person gets as many desires as possible satisfied compatible with every other person getting exactly as many desires satisfied." This principle can at first glance seem reasonable: if a person has bad luck as far as her work conditions are concerned, she might have a claim to be compensated with more money, so that she can satisfy more desires in her leisure time, than the one who can satisfy more desires in his work, for instance. But there are severe problems: how are we to individuate and count desires? Does the man who wants a green car, have one desire or two? Suppose he wants a green Chrysler – does he then have three desires? I believe that these problems are unresolvable except by arbitrary stipulation.

After all, the idea of a scale of possible satisfaction of the model sketched by Miller is better. Maybe we could revise his principle by not measuring satisfaction from the top of the scale, but from the bottom. The principle would then say that each one ought to come as far from the bottom as is compatible with everyone else reaching the same level. But this seems a bit mean. It would imply that no one should have more satisfaction than it is possible to obtain for the least fortunate member of the society, the man who cannot get much of his desires satisfied, for instance since he is handicapped or ill and has not much time left to live. This does not seem acceptable either.

So let us try another interpretation: "Satisfy all basic needs of all members of the society, and then distribute the surplus – if there is any – according to the strength of the desires of the members of the society!"

First of all we meet with the problem of measuring the strength of desires. Perhaps someone would propose that we decide the relative strength of two desires of two different persons by asking how much each of the persons would be prone to abstain from in order to satisfy her desire. But this method presupposes first that there is a roughly equal distribution already, since a rich person is presumably more prone to spend money on satisfying a desire than the poor man is. Furthermore people might be more or less fond of what they already have, so you must also have a method to decide whether or not what they are prepared to abstain from is equally valuable to them. And how do we decide this? By asking what they can forego of possible desire-satisfaction in order to keep what they have! We seem to be going round in a circle.

But let us suppose that the problem of measuring the strength of desires were solved. Is it really just to distribute the resources of society according to the strength of the desires? Someone can have a fanatic desire, a desire which is stronger than all others so that he is prepared to forego all satisfaction of other desires to meet this one. Such desires then ought to be satisfied in the first place. But let us suppose that someone has such a fanatic desire that all persons become Christian, or that another man has such a desire for a love affair with a certain woman. It does not seem as if those two desires ought to be satisfied before all other desires in the society, even if no one else has any fanatic desires which are incompatible with these mentioned.

As a matter of fact I believe that there can be something fishy about pointing to the strength of my desire as a reason that it ought to be satisfied in the first place. Traditionally people used to point to their lineage or race or sex to justify their merit to a better treatment than others. We do not accept such claims as legitimate any longer. But is the claim in name of strength of desire more legitimate?

This question must be answered with some caution. If a person has two desires and can only satisfy one of them, she will satisfy the strongest of them. This is trivially true according to the theory of action of Donald Davidson, for instance. If a friend, a parent, or someone else with a special relation to her (such as a doctor to her patient) can satisfy either of these desires for this person, she also *ceteris paribus* ought to satisfy the strongest one. In this way strength of desire is morally relevant. This is also so when we say that what is to be considered is preference orderings of possible worlds: the person who more ardently desires that x than she desires that y, would prefer the world where her desire for x but not for y was satisfied, to the world which contained y but not x. Thus a stronger desire *ceteris paribus* ought to satisfied before the weaker desire.

However, this is generally true only when we have to deal with different desires of the same person. If two or more persons are involved, the fact that one of them generally has stronger desires or aversions than the other, does not play any vital role, when considering what to do to them, or which one of them has the greater right to satisfy his desires, if they conflict. The relative strength of desires determines the preference-orders of the individuals, but we are not to assign less importance to the satisfaction of the desires of a certain person just because she happens to desire less strongly than another. Each individual is as important as every other, irrespective of whether

her desires generally are strong or weak (or if some of them are very intense). When choosing what to do, when several persons are concerned, we are to consider only the ordering of possible worlds, not the strength by which each person desires, so only the relative strength of desires within one and the same person, will be of moral importance.

On the other hand we have not as yet solved the problem of what a just distribution in terms of preference-orderings looks like. Proportionately equal contributions to each person's level of satisfaction did not seem an acceptable solution to the distribution-problem, neither did any other of the proposed solutions.

The conclusion which I will tentatively propose is that our intuitions as far as 'justice' is concerned, are rather vague, when it comes to distribution of the surplus of the society, i.e. those resources which are not necessary to satisfy basic needs. What is definitely unjust is to distribute the resources so that one person is starving to death, while others live in luxury. When we leave such problems behind we have rather vague ideas about justice. This in itself is an argument in favour of equality: if no sound reason can be given for treating individuals unequally, then they ought to be treated equally. This is just the formal element in justice which comes to the fore. This seems most akin to a requirement of consistency: if no relevant reasons can be set forth to the contrary, then two cases ought to be treated equally. That the basic needs of two persons differ, so that one of them will die unless he gets greater economic resources than the other, *is* a relevant consideration, which gives a reason for difference in treatment.

The last possibility I will consider is to combine the idea of satisfaction of needs and desires with John Rawls' Difference Principle. We would then get something like this: "Social and economic inequalities are to be arranged so that the least advantaged get as much satisfaction of needs and desires as possible." Rawls' own version is so well-known that I do not need to go into details to show in what ways my version differs from the original. John Rawls argues that rational, mutually disinterested persons behind a veil of ignorance would choose some maximin-strategy to safeguard their most vital interests. This would lead to a principle roughly stating that what is important is the state of the least well off group in society: their part of primary goods, should be as great as possible. There have been a lot of different criticisms of this idea. In some situations it prescribes too much equality, in some too little. And his idea of making the distribution of primary goods the criterion of justice is not quite acceptable either. One type of situation where his theory would prescribe too much equality, if it were applied to them, are those of extreme scarcity, where all would be pressed down below the welfare floor where life begins to be worth living. Rawls is conscious of this problem and therefore restricts his theory to situations of moderate scarcity. Another situation where Rawls' theory demands too much equality is, in my view, the situation where diminishing the share of the most fortunate does not in any way help the less fortunate, but where the inequalities are not necessary to raise the level of the least well off group. As far as I understand Rawls, his theory implies that such inequalities are not allowed: we have to cut down the riches of the fortunate ones just to make equality greater. This seems to be a little mean. As Brian Barry (1973) has pointed out the idea of primary goods is not altogether happy either, since the instrumental value of primary goods varies from society to society and from one situation to another. So you cannot say that it is always better the more you get of primary goods. The more you get of money, cars (Barry's example), housing, etc., the better – as a general rule in our type of society. But if we all get more and more money, inflation will make life very troublesome; and if we all get more and more cars, in the end no one will be able to move an inch on the roads. (Barry 1973, 116-121) Furthermore, Rawls does not take into account differences in needs, that someone because of some illness or handicap might need more primary goods than most individuals need to reach the same level of well-being. (Barry 1973, 56)

These arguments do not hit this new version of Rawls' Difference Principle. This is so, since there is a limit of need-satisfaction. If you get more resources, when your needs are satisfied, you do not get more need-satisfaction. It is rather to be believed that you can satisfy some desires. When not all can have their needs satisfied, it is better that some do, so that at least they will survive. And there are no restrictions on people's striving for desire-satisfaction as long as they do not exploit others or use for themselves means that others also want. But the mere fact that they are better off is not unacceptable according to my theory.

However, there is something sound in the efforts of the persons in the original position of Rawls to safeguard their most vital interests. 1966 Nicholas Rescher proposed a kind of insurance-strategy:

> Actual privation offends our sense of justice in a more serious way than do mere inequalities.
> These considerations suggest adding to the principle of utility another qualifying clause, a "principle of catastrophe-prevention" stipulating a minimal utility floor for all individuals below which no one should be pressed. (Rescher 1966, 29)

My proposal that the need-satisfaction of all shall take precedence over the satisfaction of desire is an example of such an insurance strategy, while Rescher himself does not spell out this idea, but instead tries to give a mathematical formula for measuring acceptable inequality, a formula which does not yield acceptable results (cf Pontara 1985).

James P. Sterba argues that the persons in Rawls' original position would rather choose some kind of insurance strategy than the principles proposed by Rawls. Thus he argues that they would state a principle that first all needs should be satisfied and then the surplus, if there were one, would be distributed according to some Nozickian principle:

> *Principle of Need.* Each person is guaranteed the primary social goods that are necessary to meet the normal costs of satisfying his basic needs in the society in which he lives.
> *Principle of Appropriation and Exchange.* Additional primary social goods are to be distributed on the basis of private appropriation and voluntary agreement and exchange. (Sterba 1980, 55)[12]

To these two principles Sterba adds a principle of minimal contribution, and a principle of just savings for future generations, and principles of retributive justice. In this context however I just want to point to the basic idea that justice means that as many as possible get their basic needs met. What makes utilitarianism and Nozick's theory of free appropriation and exchange seem outrageously unjust is not that they permit very great inequalities under certain circumstances, but that these inequalities can mean that one human being is denied the most elementary prerequisites of a human life, while others can dwell in luxury. Such possible consequences of an ethical theory make many philosophers formulate restrictions to make sure that their theories will not permit outcomes of that kind.

Traditionally the opinion has been that the formal principle of justice needs a complement, telling which differences are morally relevant: difference in merit, rights, or needs have been answers to that question. I have tried to give reasons showing that differences in needs are relevant to the question about just distribution only in so far as basic needs are

---

[12] As far as I can see the arguments given by Sterba tell equally well in favour of changing the last-mentioned principle for a principle of distribution according to merit: Sterba writes about the importance that the efforts of people should give some result, etc.

concerned. Under other interpretations the principle "to each according to his needs" does not give any clear and reasonable answer. This in its turn seems to me to indicate that the idea behind the principle of needs is some idea about all individuals' equal rights to the possibility of living a good life.

I have an interest in my own happiness, but I have a right only to pursue it. Only those interests are rights which other people can do something to secure, and which it is desirable for the moral code of society to be invoked in securing. (Brandt 1983, 44)

Taken together the arguments point towards an idea that what is important from the moral point of view is that each individual is guaranteed an acceptable life and as far as possible equal pre-requisite conditions to live a good life. But this points in the direction of a theory of rights rather than a theory of justice. When a distribution clearly seems unjust, it is because it violates some rights rather than that it shows a particular pattern of distribution. Therefore I sketch a theory of rights in Ch. 6.

'Need' as a bridge between 'is' and 'ought'

For those who want to commit the naturalistic fallacy, it is tempting to start out with some concept of 'need'. 'Need' takes a place in between empirical and normative concepts. A need-statement is empirical – its truth-value is decided by empirical methods – but at the same time it seems to imply a legitimate claim. Many philosophers have taken this characteristic of need-statements to indicate that the border between fact and norm is not after all so watertight as has been supposed.

We would for example hesitate to call the rapist's desire to rape a certain woman a need, since we would not accept that he ought to get his desire satisfied. This characteristic of 'need' lies behind the attempts of Kai Nielsen, David Miller, and Knut Erik Tranøy to make need-statements immune against normative critique by making normatively relevant features part of the definition of "need". I have tried to avoid explicit normative conditions on the concept of 'need' defined in Ch. 5. But there certainly is some connection between needs and norms, but what is this connection?

Georg Henrik von Wright and Garrett Thomson seem to hold a general naturalistic meta-ethics, when analysing "need". von Wright is of the opinion that "the beneficial and the harmful and the good of man set the conceptual frame for 'a moral point of view'" (von Wright, 1963 II, vi). These concepts in turn are related to "the needs and wants of individual men". (*Ibid.*) And you might remember that he takes the good of man to be empirically observable (cf pp 46f above). Garrett Thomson comes close to the standpoint of von Wright, when he argues that what is good for men is decided by their interests, which in turn can be objectively ascertained as a kind of basic psychological (or physiological?) properties of men. According to Thomson, as you might remember, we have needs of that which is necessary to avoid harm, i.e. to avoid the frustration of vital interests.

Kai Nielsen and Knut Erik Tranøy take the connection between 'need' and 'ought' to be non-contingent, although not strictly logical or semantical. Nielsen's idea is that statements about needs pragmatically imply normative statements; it would be "logically odd" to deny that needs ought to be satisfied (Nielsen, 1963 and 1969). Tranøy (1972-75) tries to establish a meta-norm as "unrejectable": 'ought' implies 'can'; therefore no norm requiring the impossible can be valid. From this idea Tranøy goes on to establish the "Bridge Principle" – the unrejectable meta-norm making it possible to derive valid norms concerning human rights. One version of this principle runs as follows: "If p is known by *b* to be necessary for *a* then it is not permitted for *b* to forbid *a* to do p." (Tranøy 1975, 147)[13]

Statements about needs are statements about what is necessary to individuals. They *must* satisfy their needs. Therefore they cannot be under an obligation to do anything which comes into conflict with their satisfaction of needs. Tranøy believes that the Bridge Principle therefore "gives rise to or generates corresponding human rights" (Tranøy 1975, 147). But the needs are to be satisfied iff certain goals are to be reached, so there is no strict necessity involved. It is necessary to satisfy basic needs to survive – but it is not necessary to survive. ("Mais il faut vivre!" – "Je ne peut pas voir cet besoin!") Furthermore in order to establish human rights to need-satisfaction, Tranøy tacitly assumes that 'forbid', 'stop', and 'not help' can be identified. But this is far from true. The football player must not forbid a player of the opposite team to shoot the ball in his goal, but he may try to stop him (shall we not say that he *ought* to do this?), and he definitely has no obligation to help him score. So even if we accept that you must not forbid anyone to

---

[13] Tranøy is influenced by von Wright's analysis of norms in *Norm and Action* (1963 I); but the idea can be stated without these ideas about norm-sender and promulgation of norms. The idea then would be that no norms ordering the impossible would be valid.

satisfy his needs, and assume that he must satisfy them (which is true only in an elliptical sense), we cannot – unfortunately – get from here to a positive obligation to help others satisfy their needs.

Plant, Lesser and Taylor-Gooby (1980) try to get around Hume's guillotine in the following way: to be able to derive 'ought' from 'has a need', there must be a normative principle which implies the norm; but in order to make the derivation normatively neutral, this normative principle should be a basic presupposition behind *all* normative systems. Thus they take need-statements to state conditions necessary to be able to follow any norms at all; thereby they think that need-statements are normatively neutral – they do not presuppose one determinate moral system – but nevertheless you can derive norms from them:

> ... there are some conditions necessary for doing anything at all, for performing any action or pursuing any goal whatsoever. No matter what morality one adopts, these conditions will be necessary for carrying it out.
> Needs of this sort must be acknowledged in all societies, whatever this moral code or standards, and may fairly be called 'unqualified' or 'human' needs'. (Plant, Lesser, & Taylor-Gooby, 1980, 37)

> ... the existence of moral agents is a necessary precondition of moral activity. So if human beings have moral duties at all, they have a need to survive, which in turn implies a duty to help each other to survive and to preserve life. One can avoid this conclusion by denying that we do have moral obligations; but such a view, although it may be irrefutable, is not actually held by any sane person, much as people may differ over what our obligations are. (*Ibid.*, 38)

In a way my own proposal is akin to that of Plant, Lesser, and Taylor-Gooby: I take satisfaction of basic needs to be a necessary condition of anything we can find valuable. The theory sketched in Ch. 1 gives a naturalistic analysis of 'value', but it also states that such a naturalism lacks moral force, since the important question in ethics is "What ought I to do?" And this question is not automatically answered when we know what has intrinsic value. To give a naturalistic analysis of norms is much more difficult than to do the same thing concerning 'value'. However, I tried to show that moral norms could be taken as institutionalized rules expressing the claims of individuals. Both the institution of ethical rules and their main contents could be explained by our needs and desires. Thus in a way 'need' *is* a link between facts and norms.

It seems to me that the moral importance of needs consists in the fact that morals must have some connection with human nature and the conditions of man. Every living being has needs which must be satisfied if she is to survive and be able to satisfy any interests. I have therefore chosen to define 'basic needs' as those conditions that must obtain if we are to have an acceptable life, which is a prerequisite – as far as we know – of everything that is important to human beings and animals. 'An acceptable life' can be considered too value-infected a concept to be used to define a purely empirical concept. But I have tried to make clear which conditions must obtain if someone is to have an acceptable life, and if my account is accepted, it is clearly an empirical question to decide whether these conditions obtain or not. In a way I have made a value-biased definition, but it seems to me that it is a rather innocuous definition nonetheless: almost all human beings can agree that the satisfaction of needs thus defined is of immense importance. Thus basic needs can be taken to constitute a kind of rock-bottom of morals.

On the other hand basic needs thus defined must play different roles in different moral frame-works. To a confirmed utilitarian needs can at most find a place in rules of thumb pointing out important means of achieving the utilitarian good, the greatest happiness of the greatest number. But in a moral frame-work designed to safe-guard human autonomy, where the good life is taken to be the free pursuit of whatever goal we choose, basic needs must play a much more central role. Where respect rather than maximization of happiness is central, the right to need-satisfaction will be the first and last injunction of morals (together with the prescription that we ought not to interfere with the pursuit of others, unless they thereby threaten vital interests of other people). Thus in the theory of rights sketched in the last chapter, the right to need-satisfaction will be of prime importance.

Chapter 4

Desires

This chapter will discuss what kinds of attitudes are to be ascribed moral relevance. In the first chapter I proposed that intrinsic desires make up one kind of morally relevant interest. I will first state what I mean by "desire", then discuss some conditions which it has traditionally been supposed must obtain if desires are to have moral relevance. By "moral relevance" I here refer to two different conceptions: first I want to consider some conditions which have been proposed by philosophers, who, like me, have been positive to the idea that desire-satisfaction is what ultimately has moral importance, in which case "moral relevance" can be taken to be the same as "intrinsic value". But since I am sceptical towards the traditional concept of intrinsic value and its function in morals, I am primarily interested in the question whether these conditions seem relevant to sort out those attitudes which we would like to see safeguarded by social rules stating that we have a right to strive to satisfy them. Lastly I will discuss some problems for such an alternative to a theory of "value".

When talking about desires I refer to a wide spectrum of positive and negative attitudes.[1] There are a lot of words, with slightly different meanings: "want", "desire", "lust", "wish", "striving", "longing", "preference", "like", "dislike", "abhorrence", etc., which all refer to

---

[1] So does Ralph Barton Perry but he calls such attitudes "interests": "...*this state, act or disposition of favor or disfavor,* to which we propose to give the name of '*interest*'." (1926; quotation from 1950, 115.) As I understand Perry, the concept his term "interest" covers is the same as the one I want to call desire. (My own use of "interest" includes not only attitudes of favour or disfavour, but also the necessary conditions for obtaining what we desire and avoiding what we shun.)

phenomena of the kind I want to include in the class of desires. You can make a lot of subtle distinctions between different kinds of positive and negative attitudes which do not matter in this context. Every kind of positive or negative attitude is reckoned morally relevant as long as they fulfil the conditions to be stated in what follows.

Desires as behaviour dispositions

But we must clarify somewhat what is meant by "positive or negative attitudes", or, in short, "desires". I use the term "desires" to refer to some kind of behavioural dispositions. The idea is worked out in the works of Donald Davidson, for instance. Richard Brandt has used this way of analysing "desire" in moral contexts. I will take his analysis as a starting point:

> We shall therefore say that a person 'wants' something O, or that something O "is valenced for" him at the time, if his central motive state is such that if it were then to occur to him that a certain act of his then would tend to bring O about, his tendency to perform that act would be increased. (Brandt 1979, 26)

I propose a revised version of Brandt's definition:
> A desires x, iff A is in such a state that if it then occurred to A, that she could bring x about, and she had no contrary desires, then A's tendency to try to bring x about (whether through an intentional action or some kind of reflex behaviour) would increase.

My reasons for the changes are the following. That "person" is replaced by "A" is motivated by my want not to delimit the class of morally relevant desires to human desires. If "occur" is interpreted cognitively in a strong sense, animals will nevertheless be excluded. "Occur to" therefore in this context does not imply that x has a conscious thought with propositional content. A cat e.g. can imagine food in his bowl and behave in an appropriate way – rub himself against my legs – to bring it about that food is placed in the bowl, and this does not imply that the cat has any thoughts with propositional content, although you can truly say of the cat that "it seems as if he wants food". If we have strong requirements on what to count as an action, animals will be excluded anyhow. Therefore I have added that the relevant behaviour tendencies include forms of reflex behaviour. Of course it can also be true of human beings that they close their eyes for example to shut out too strong a light. And we can say that we want to shut the light out, although the behaviour is caused by a reflex. The clause about contrary desires is inserted to provide for desires that are outweighed by stronger desires to the contrary. Someone can desire a certain necklace, it can occur to him that he can steal it, but his tendency to perform the theft is blocked by his fear of being captured by the police. There are wishes which we never try to fulfill, because the satisfaction of our desires would inevitably lead to consequences we definitely not want to bring about. But in that case we *would* try to satisfy our desires *were* we certain that the consequences would not follow.²

But are there not weaker sorts of wishes, which cannot be analysed in terms of dispositions to act? Can it not be true that you wish to cut someone's ears off, although you never make an attempt, even in situations where it would be possible? Such wishes are excluded by my definition. The reason is that wishes which are so impotent, that you don't even try to satisfy them in situations when it would be possible, seem not to be urgent enough to be morally relevant.

A disposition analysis of "desire" has to deal with some problems, among them the following. A neurotic with compulsive behaviour shows several times a day that his most dominant desire is to wash his hands. Nevertheless we would say that his desire to get rid of his compulsive behaviour is more important. This is motivated by the fact that he has to give up so much – reading books, meeting other people, making love, going to the cinema. Still his behaviour shows that his desire to wash his hands is stronger than all his other desires. If he seeks psychiatric treatment, we would encourage him and try to get him to keep to his purpose to go to the consultation at the appointed time (*if* we believed that the treatment would have the intended effect). What are we to say about this case? We can assume that the neurotic has a second order – although not stronger – desire to get rid of his compulsive behaviour. We ought to pay greater attention to this desire because this is what the neurotic himself would do, if he had it in his power. Thus it is not enough just to take those desires into account that in practice appear strongest – we must compare them to the desires the person himself would satisfy if he had it in is power and were fully informed (including not only cognitive knowledge but also experience), i.e. the analysis of "desire" in terms of "dispositions" is just a preliminary step

---

² Some of these ideas are inspired by a correspondence with Dan Egonson, who has formulated a utilitarian theory based on interest satisfaction (Egonson 1990). The same is true of parts of the rest of the discussion about the concept of 'desire'.

in the delimiting of a class of morally relevant "desires": there are more conditions that have to be met for a desire to be morally relevant.

Another problem, however, which directly concerns the analysis in terms of dispositions to act, which Egonsson points out (but does not solve satisfactorily: Egonson 1990, 67-68) is the following: let us assume that I wake up in a house on fire; I have a desperate desire to escape the flames, but the very strength of my desire paralyses me, so that I can do nothing to get away. Are there any ways of saving the disposition analysis in this case? Egonsson tries two ways: either you take the inactivity in itself as an expression of my desperate desire, or you conclude that after all I do not want to escape. The latter proposal goes against the assumptions – we can take for granted that I really do want to escape. And the former solution seems odd, because it makes it impossible to distinguish between someone who does desire to escape, and someone who does not, unless we can discern some difference between the two cases – perhaps the desperate man stretches his muscles so that he cannot move, while the one who wants to die, waits quiet and relaxed for the end. Even if we consider desires as broadly dispositional – i.e. they can be manifested in many different actions: the man in the burning house can run to the door, open the window, scream for help and so forth – you must be able to discern some difference between the man wanting to escape and the man who does not. But it is not certain that there will be any external differences to be apprehended, there might not be any discernible differences to the observer. The difference however might be observed "from the inside" so to say. That means that you must not be too rigidly behaviouristic in the conception of "behaviour tendency": it might be the case that the decision and the attempt to get away is something that in some cases can only be observed by the man himself. On the other hand, in some other cases, the observer might be able to know better the real motives and desires of a man than the man himself. This means that the individual who has the desire is not always and in principle accorded a privileged position when it comes to knowing his own desires. Maybe this is all we want from a disposition analysis of desire. (Cf Egonsson 1990, 69.)[3]

---

[3] It might seem as if the permanently paralysed person would pose an even greater problem for the dispositional analysis of desires, but I do not think so. The analysis says that if it were to occur to A that the desired state *could be brought about* by some action, then A:s tendency to perform this action would increase. And this is true also of the paralysed: *if* he came to believe that a wink or some other action of his would bring the desired state about, he would try to perform this action.

When it comes to inadequate reactions by animals – the small hare lies down instead of running from the cat, the horse turns back and runs into the burning stable – it is easier to defend the disposition analysis: the animals "act" in the way they take by instinct or habit to be the safest way.

A third problem is posed by *akrasia*, "weakness of will": "the good that I would I do not: but the evil which I would not, that I do" (S:t Paul in Rom. 7.19.). If this was true of S:t Paul then you couldn't take his actions as true expressions of his wants. On the other hand I believe that you can assume that S:t Paul is not quite sincere: he wants both the good thing and the bad one – but the latter desire is the stronger one. That he does not believe this himself might be explained in the following way: he has a second order desire that he should not desire the evil and this desire is the one with which he identifies himself. A man wants to quit smoking. He sincerely wants this, and he tries hard. But all the same he takes a cigarette when offered, he eagerly looks for lost cigarette-boxes with some cigarettes left and so forth. I believe that we have to say that this man has two wants: he wants to quit smoking, and he wants to smoke. If his desire to quit is sincere and he takes some steps to realize this want, he feels ashamed when he takes a smoke, and so forth, I would say that this desire is the most important one even if his desire to smoke is the stronger one. This is so because he has a second order desire not to want to smoke. And second order desires as a rule must be ascribed more moral relevance than first order desires, since the former ones express the well-considered autonomous desires of the person. (In this respect I diverge from the opinion of Egonson who always takes the strongest desire to be the one to be satisfied, *ceteris paribus*.)

A fourth problem is the phenomenon of depression. A very depressed person has no goal worthy of the least exertion. Nothing can get her to leave her bed. The world has lost its colour. Such a woman does not live a good life – she would be better off if she had some desires. As far as I understand, a state of depression is conceived as very painful – so the depressed person has at least one desire: to get out of this state. If she were offered a pill which with certainty would get her out of her depression, she would take it. If her depression is so deep that she couldn't even get herself to do this, I believe that a good guess based on information from people who have been deeply depressed, is that such a state is so bad, that we ought to try to cure it, by electric shocks, medicine or in any way effective.

A fifth problem is connected with positive and negative attitudes which are not actualized until you have had certain experiences. You can eat a dish without any desire beforehand and realize that you like the taste. You can smell the fragrance of a flower hitherto unknown to you and find that you like it. I presume, however, that such attitudes in the future will give rise to action-tendencies under certain conditions. And they do not differ from most of our desires in this respect: we learn what to desire by experience. At first you like simple pop-music and dislike classic music; your friends take you to concerts and to the opera; you fake some interest, and after a while you may come to like it. If your newly acquired likings were to fade away with more experience (or greater self-confidence) then they are not reckoned as your real ones, but if they stay stable they are to be accounted relevance. I propose that we call immediate attitudes of liking, simply "likes", and ascribe them – as well as acquired desires and likes – moral relevance under the same conditions as the rest.

I conclude that the problems with the disposition analysis of 'desire' are not insurmountable.

Intrinsic desires

In this wide field of positive and negative attitudes you can distinguish between constant and more transient desires, between occurring and dormant desires, between permanent desires and whims. Unconscious desires are presupposed in psychoanalytic tradition, and so forth. But I will consider just two distinctions that may be of importance in normative contexts, the distinction between intrinsic and instrumental desires, and the distinction between self-related desires and those that concern others.

It is usually taken for granted that it is the intrinsic desires – if any – that are morally relevant. "Intrinsic desires" is taken to mean that the desires are directed towards states wanted in themselves – not as means to further ends. Now I am not quite sure that this distinction is so clear cut as is generally believed. I prefer one special path on my way to my work: a path winding through a park along a narrow creek. Is this preference intrinsic or instrumental? Riding this path by bike is of course a means to get to my work. But my preference for this path before other possible ways (among which some are shorter) is not instrumental, or so it seems to me. You could possibly say that taking this path is a means of getting intrinsically desired experiences: looking at the boats, smelling the fragrance of the bird-cherry in the spring and so forth. Even though I might not intrinsically desire to look at the boats and smell the bird-cherry, I do intrinsically *prefer* this to looking at cars and smelling exhaust-gas. Now this might be true, but I believe that it is very difficult to discern those elements of my experiences on my way to work that are intrinsically desired (or preferred) from those that are only instrumentally desired. I would rather think that some of the experiences tend to contribute to making my day better. Many things are desired as parts of a whole situation: it is nice to sit in front of a burning fire on a chilly autumn day listening to the wind in the treetops. Both the fire and the wind contribute to making you feel cosy. If it were not so chilly and windy, the fire would not be so attractive, and without the fire in a warm room the wind and the cold are not very pleasant either. It seems to be the combination, the total situation, that makes you feel comfortable. Therefore it seems as if we often desire states and things because they would contribute to making a total situation attractive. Such contributive values seem to be of greater importance when we think about how to act, than are considerations about intrinsically desirable states. There might in other words be "organic wholes" in the sense used by G.E. Moore, where the parts have no value, or even negative value, but which nevertheless contribute to making a whole situation intrinsically desirable. (Cf also C.I. Lewis 1950, 488-495.)

However, I will not make a point of this, because it is possible that you could think in the following way: the parts of a total situation which I have found it plausible to call contributively valuable, may have a fixed value, *given* the situation. If so you could say that they have a definite intrinsic value in each situation, but that the value varies with the situation.[4] Perhaps no stronger thesis can be defended. And then it seems plausible to argue that d, as a part of the total situation S1 has the intrinsic value $v1$, although d, as part of another situation S2 would have had a different intrinsic value, $v2$. I will in what follows write about intrinsic desires as if this was unproblematic. But you ought to keep in mind that among intrinsic desires are reckoned both intrinsic preferences and some desires and preferences that might be more correctly described as desires and preferences for things and states motivated by their capacity to contribute to intrinsic desirability of other more complex states.

---

[4] This is not G.E. Moore's idea of intrinsic value, since he takes the criterion of the intrinsic goodness of x to be that it would be good if x existed quite alone. He is therefore forced to introduce organic wholes to deal with such cases.

Self-related desires

It has often been argued that the only desires that ought to be taken into consideration in moral contexts are the self-interested desires, i.e. desires that I have concerning states which I want for my own sake. Altruistic and malevolent desires, i.e. desires that others should do or experience something that does not directly concern me, are taken to be irrelevant from the moral point of view. (Cf e.g. Overvold, cited in Brandt 1979, 329.) One reason is that if I want something to be true of you, which you do not desire, it seems unreasonable that my want in any way should be relevant when it comes to the question of what should be done to you. Many persons have strong desires concerning the actions of others, often when it does not seem to be their business. Let us assume for instance that a majority of people abhor the thought of homosexual activities. They strongly desire that no one should take part in such activities. These acts in no way influence the lives of the heterosexual majority. Would it not be absurd to require that homosexuals should abstain from physical love just to satisfy the desires of the majority? The missionary wants the heathen people to accept Christianity – does this ardent desire confer any moral obligation on the heathens to become Christians?

A further reason is that if altruistic desires are ascribed moral relevance, some persons' interests will be counted twice as it were. The welfare of queen Silvia of Sweden would be much more important than the welfare of my old mother, since there are thousands of persons who desire the welfare of the queen, while there are comparatively few persons concerned about the welfare of my mother. Thus allowing all kinds of desires to be counted, seems to be in conflict with the principle of Bentham: "Each to count for one, and none for more than one."

But why not count all desires, on the other hand, each for one and none for more than one? I believe that many individuals would prefer contributing to the welfare of the queen rather than to their own – it might seem irrational, but if they would still do so, when fully informed, what should we say? I want my children to be happy and if I had to choose I would rather see that they were happy than that I was. This would be the desire I would try to satisfy. If that is true, then, according to the argument presented in Ch. 1, this is the desire that someone else would be obliged to satisfy for me, *ceteris paribus*. And it is not impossible that someone would prefer that the desires of the royal children were satisfied rather than those of her own children. It might seem improbable that such a want would persist when she were fully informed, but *if* it were to persist, why not acknowledge it as morally relevant?

Thus there seem to be reasons both for and against awarding the distinction between self-related desires and other desires moral relevance. However, this is of no great importance as far as the ethical system sketched in Ch. 6 is concerned, since according to that system what is morally required is to satisfy the needs of others. Mere desires are of less importance: we have no general obligation to strive for the satisfaction of the desires of others, unless bound to them by personal ties, explicit undertakings or suchlike. What is required is that we do not interfere with the strivings of others, unless their strivings threaten the vital interests of others. Therefore the heathens are under no obligation to satisfy the desire of the missionary, nor are the homosexuals under any obligation to satisfy the desires of the prejudiced majority.

When it comes to the desires of someone we love or someone we have promised to help, all other things being equal, it is more important to satisfy a strong desire than a weaker one, simply because this is the choice I would make myself, if my desires came into conflict. Thus if someone ought to do to me what I want him to do, he should satisfy my strongest desire. This however is complicated by the fact that the neurotic in his behaviour shows that his strongest desire is to wash his hands. Now I believe that this problem can be solved if we assume that the neurotic would rather want to satisfy other desires if he could – his neurosis makes it impossible for him to satisfy any other desires than the impulse to wash his hands. But if he had it in his power he would rather do other things. This is further strengthened by the assumption that we ought to pay greater attention to second order desires than to those of the first order.

There is one context, however, where the distinction between self-related desires and other desires seems to play a role: I propose in Ch. 6 that individuals should be free to strive for their own goals as long as they do not interfere with the strivings of others. In that context it seems as if the distinction is of some importance, since it seems more important that your desires concerning your own life ought to have greater weight than some other person's desires concerning *your* life. Thus if two desires conflict on whether P should do *a* or *b*, P wanting to do *a* and S wanting P to do *b*, and the consequences of *a* and *b* only affect P, then the desire of P ought to take precedence.

Informed desires

Are we to suppose that all intrinsic desires are equally morally relevant provided that they are equal in strength? Even those liberals that tend to dig up the hatchet and grind it when hearing about "true interests" and suchlike are usually willing to delimit the class of morally relevant desires somewhat more narrowly by requiring some condition of rationality or well-informedness to be fulfilled.

The condition is formulated in different ways by different authors: Sidgwick wants the desires to be "in harmony with reason" (Sidgwick 1966, 112); Richard Brandt 1979 reckons only those desires that would survive "cognitive psychotherapy"; Richard Hare considers "what they would desire if they were fully informed and unconfused" (Hare 1981, 28); Harsanyi talks about "true preferences", explained in the following way:

> [...A] person's true preferences are the preferences he *would* have if he had all the relevant factual information, always reasoned with the greatest possible care, and were in a state of mind most conducive to rational choice. (Harsanyi 1982, 55)

These are just a few exponents of the idea – Peter Singer, Georg Henrik von Wright and many others also subscribe to some condition of rationality.

Dan Egonson is, as far as I know, the only one who does not accept any such condition. His arguments (Egonson 1990, 94-115) boil down to the following:
a) information and clear thinking are important first and foremost when instrumental desires are concerned; but what is morally relevant is the satisfaction of intrinsic desires, and these are to a much lesser degree influenced by information and logic; b) if we take just desires a person *would have* if fully informed, etc., it might be the case that some actual desires were not rational in this sense; we would then be obliged to satisfy hypothetical desires of people, desires they *do not* have. This seems strange to Egonsson.

To this comes a further argument to the effect that we would hardly ever know what to do to others, if we were to consider what they *would desire* when fully informed, etc. But this seems not to be a valid argument to a utilitarian: few utilitarians would say that we *know* in concrete circumstances what to do.

But the first two arguments seem to be worthy of consideration. The first one seems not to be true, though. In many cases intrinsic desires can be affected by information, at least if "information" is taken in a wide sense, including experience and vivid imagination of what a certain state would really be like. This is stressed by Brandt among others and I believe that he is right. It might be true for instance that you would not want to go to Bangkok, if you had been there, or really knew what it is like. Certain other desires might be different if we knew the causes behind them, if we knew for example which experiences in our childhood made us desire these things, etc. And it seems to me that if we became disappointed in having a desire satisfied, then this would indicate (but does not conclusively prove) that the desire was not well-informed: we believed that this was what we desired, but as matter of fact we did not.

The second argument is more difficult. It does not seem morally urgent to satisfy merely hypothetical desires, which no one actually has. Let us assume, for instance, that someone *would* desire *x*, *if* exposed to cognitive psychotherapy of the Brandtian brand. But as a matter of fact he will never be exposed to it, and he does not want to be. So he never actually has this desire. It seems odd to say that we would be obliged to satisfy this hypothetical desire. On the other hand it seems to me quite unacceptable to take every desire as morally relevant, even if it would not survive confrontation with true information and actual experience. My reason is that I believe that what we do want, if we ponder the problem, is that our well-informed desires should be satisfied. That we want our actual desires satisfied depends on the fact that we believe them to be well-informed. If we become convinced that they are not, they will in most cases disappear. Of course we also have desires which we consider not well-informed but which nonetheless are difficult to get rid of, as is well-known by every smoker who has tried to quit smoking. But in such cases we usually have second order desires, which we believe are well-informed and which we want to gain victory over the desire to smoke.

I propose that we should not say for instance that your desires are uninformed, in those cases when *if* you had learnt something at school, or if your childhood experiences had been different, you would have had different desires. If you cannot change them now, we must take them for granted. And it must not be that what is required is a long learning process. If my son for instance wants a record with the Beatles for Christmas, and I presume that after several years of listening to music he would prefer Bach to the Beatles, I have no obligation to give him Bach instead of the Beatles. If on the other hand it is true that it is just because he happens never to have listened to any music by Bach that he wants the Beatles, and it would suffice to let him hear the mass in Bminor to get him prefer Bach to the Beatles, then it seems reasonable to say that Bach is what he really prefers.

I therefore propose that morally relevant desires have to meet two conditions: that they are actual and that they would not change if the bearer were exposed to relevant and true information or had certain experiences (which he is able to get now). You could object and say: What if there are no such desires? Someone might have no desires that meet both conditions.

What are we then to do to him? Should we satisfy his actual or his hypothetical desires? I believe that this depends upon our relationship to him. If you have a personal relationship to him it seems most reasonable to try to change his desires by giving him relevant information or by making him have the relevant experiences. In most cases lack of information and inadequate desires based on such lack justifies an attempt to inform him rather than act paternalistically by giving him things that he would appreciate if fully informed. Only in situations where urgent haste is necessary and very much is at stake – as when the suicide is already in the water – can paternalistic behaviour be justified: you ought to pull him out of the water and make him think through his problems once more.

If your relationship is not personal, you must usually take the desires of the other person for granted, as long as they are not directly and immediately harmful: you might stop a car driver from going onto an unsafe bridge even by force, if necessary. But these examples indicate that what is important in relation to persons whom we do not have a personal relationship to is safe-guarding their need-satisfaction. We can depend upon the fact that need-satisfaction is necessary to everyone: therefore we try to pull the suicide from the water and stop the driver from going onto the dangerous bridge. When it comes to the desires of strangers, I cannot see that they play any important role in moral considerations besides the fact that you ought not to interfere unless their desire-satisfaction comes into conflict with the desire-satisfaction of others. In that case the desires which would stay stable after full information are the ones that ought to be taken into contemplation. So, for instance, if a stranger asks you for the way to some address you ought to give correct information, unless this conflicts with the interests of others.

Suppose a man wants to have a vanilla ice cream. In the shop he gets to know that chocolate ice cream is cheaper. He now buys chocolate ice cream. Didn't he want vanilla ice cream? Yes, certainly, but he still more wanted to have a chocolate ice cream and save money. Orders of preference between more inclusive states of the world can be more or less well-informed too.

An objection to allowing knowledge be a criterion of which desires ought to be satisfied, is the following – in doing so you favour individuals who are rational and experienced before those less rational etc. But the criterion for a desire to be taken seriously is not that it is as a matter of fact based on true information and personal experience, but that it would not change if more information was provided. And first and foremost the degree of moral importance is a function not of the degree of well-informedness – the importance is a function of the urgency of the desire: a man can have the most well-reasoned preferences based on years of experience concerning trivial matters, and know nothing about what is important. Many persons with limited experience and lack of knowledge might nonetheless know themselves sufficiently well and be imaginative enough to have durable desires. By the way you can *happen* to have the same desires you would have if more informed. It is of course often a matter of degree whether a desire would survive information and experience, the distinction is not a clear-cut dichotomy.

Are these conditions enough to delimit the class of morally relevant desires? I have seldom met with any other conditions in the literature, but as a matter of fact I do not believe that they are the only ones that we ought to require that a desire is to meet in order to be morally relevant. This becomes especially clear if we not only consider the concept of 'moral relevance' in an unanalysed sense, but think of my argument in favour of ascribing moral relevance to desire-satisfaction. Which desires would I myself try to satisfy? Well, I would try to satisfy those desires that I actually happened to have of course (and among these I want my second-order desires satisfied in the first line). But if I was convinced that they were not well-informed I would be more cautious, I would try to get more information and experience and so forth. But this is not enough. I believe that I also would hesitate to satisfy a certain desire if I was convinced that it was the result of hypnosis or certain other forms of manipulation as well.

Further conditions

In the restaurant I order meat from wild boar. I eat it with pleasure. Then someone tells me that when we visited a variety show yesterday, a conjurer had hypnotized me, so that I today would go to a restaurant and order wild boar. I remember that I had on earlier occasions tried meat from wild boar and disliked the taste. So it must be a result of the hypnosis that today I wanted wild boar. Is it reasonable to say that it was my own desire that made me order it? Even if I do not regret my choice or find the dish distasteful after the information, I do not think that we should call this one of my genuine desires.

Let me change the example slightly. I go to a clinic to get hypnotic treatment for my desire to smoke. When I now refuse an offered Camel, I would say that this is a result of my second order desire not to want to smoke, which in turn is a result of my well-informed desire to quit smoking. If I have decided to go to a clinic to get a treatment to get rid of my smoking habit, I would say that this want of mine is of higher order, it is so to say the desire I identify myself with. But this is not true of my desire to eat wild boar pork. I have not come to an agreement with the hypnotist, let us assume, to get rid of my distaste for wild boar. Therefore my ordering of wild boar is not an expression of my morally relevant desires. The same is true of certain other kinds of manipulation, such as chemical or electric intervention in the central nervous system and some kinds of intense propaganda and "brainwashing". It is on the other hand difficult to distinguish some manipulation by advertising and propaganda from more legitimate ways of influencing attitudes and evaluations. I believe that we – *pace* Marcuse – should say that propaganda that is really effective, i.e. which really changes the attitudes of someone, does not make the desires less relevant.[1] If a person has undergone some change, so that she now has different desires from those she had earlier – why deny that these desires ought to be satisfied? If she really desires something it doesn't matter how she came to have the desire. This is true even if the desire is the result of intentional manipulation from someone else. Education is for instance intended to change the preferences and desires of the pupils. If it succeeds, then the desires are changed. No human being would be truly human without any kind of education. You could even compare with the case of needs: if someone lacks one leg as a result of some violent act of another, you wouldn't deny that this man now needs a wooden leg.

So the problem with hypnosis and brainwashing is not so much that desires are changed by illegitimate methods, but that we believe that such desires are easily changed, if not by more information so by other easily performed actions: if the hypnotist wakes his victim, or if the brainwashed person is treated in a familiar milieu etc. The same is true of desires influenced by drugs. When the drug ceases to have effect, the desire has gone. On the other hand some such changes might be more difficult to bring about: the drug addict might have to go through a long

---

[1] This seems to be the position of Richard Brandt too: Brandt 1979, 113.

period of abstinence or gradual withdrawal of the drug, to get back to his normal state. The reason why we say nonetheless that what we ought to do for the drug-addict is to make him quit taking drugs, is that his well-informed second-order desires say (or would say) that this is what is most in his interest, because being a drug-addict means that you must forego the satisfaction of so many important desires: to live a long and healthy life, to have a satisfactory family life, etc.

The situation is complicated by the fact that there are certain individuals who need some drug to be "normal", e.g. the diabetic needs some extra insulin to be normal. Likewise if a drug addict tells us that his mental state under the influence of mescaline is the true state, while the square consciousness of the average American is narrow and limited, how are we to decide whether he is right or not? There are other difficult borderline cases exemplified by the victims of certain fanatical sects, which more or less brainwash their members. When such a victim is kidnapped by her parents and brainwashed back into normality – is she brought back to her "true self" or not?

There are some further conditions that can influence desires in peculiar ways, such as lack of need satisfaction. Some pregnant women have rather bizarre desires for food due to some deficit in their need satisfaction. If you could find out what their needs were and satisfy them, their peculiar desires would presumably fade away. Such desires need not be taken as true desires, but rather as signs of some lack or deficit.

I will not make the distinction between morally relevant desires and those that are not in terms of rationality or moral legitimacy; I want to distinguish between desires that are difficult to change and those that are not. If some desires are impossible to change, you cannot ask whether it would be better to change the desires or to satisfy them (cf Thomson 1987, 85f). Those desires that you cannot change *are* in a way you: they are what must motivate your actions and strivings.[2] You want to be able to satisfy your well-informed desires. So do I. So I have to respect your striving, since I want the same respect from you.

In recent times a new problem has appeared for a theory that says that what is intrinsically valuable is satisfaction of unchangeable desires: in the future it might be possible to change desires by genetic

---

[2] It might seem queer that we ought to respect the strivings of the murderer Johannes in C.J.L. Almquist's *Amorina*, who has an irresistible drive to taste human blood. But I believe that *if* his desire could be satisfied without molesting other people, he would have a right to strive for satisfaction.

manipulation. Thus even if some desires are genetically determined we cannot say that they are unchangeable, in principle no desires will be unchangeable. In that case how are we to evaluate changes of desires? This question has already been touched upon in Ch. 2. Just let me recapitulate the results of that discussion.

In some such cases it seems to me that we ought to take the second order desires of the individual himself to be decisive. *If* a fully informed man wants to undergo a treatment that would change some of his desires, e.g. his desire for alcohol or his desire to rape small girls, it seems reasonable to take his second order desires about his own desires to be the morally relevant ones, the ones he identifies with and wants satisfied. If someone were to want some other kind of change – he wants no longer to feel sympathy with the unfortunate ones (he has read Nietzsche and wants to become Superman) – this might be morally relevant, if this change is compatible with other desires this man and his fellow creatures have. (Which does, however, seem rather implausible!) In some rare cases – Jack the Ripper and the murderer Johannes – someone's desires can be changed in the interests of others. The desires someone will have after treatment of the genes will of course not be morally relevant until the treatment has been successfully performed. But suppose that such a treatment is rather drastic and would change the whole personality of the individual treated? Let us assume that a person suffering from Mongolism or a schizophrenic can get their genes repaired so that they become "normal", then it must be very difficult to know if their wants as to whether they should undergo the treatment or not *can* be wellinformed.

Summary

An individual has at the time t, a morally relevant desire that x, if and only if:
a) she desires or likes that x at t;
b) this desire or like would not change as a result of increased knowledge or experience;
c) the desire or like is not the result of hypnosis or drugs (except such drugs which are necessary for her normal functioning; as far as hypnosis is concerned the condition is that she has not come to an agreement with the hypnotist about some treatment that is in accordance with her own higher order desires);
d) she is not at t brainwashed or manipulated with regard to this desire or like in a way which could be changed by more information or some kind of deindoctrination.

As far as desires changed by genetic manipulation are concerned they are reckoned morally relevant after the change has taken place, whether they are chosen by herself or not, if the change is irrevocable. When it comes to animals, I believe that the conditions must be changed in this way:
An animal, A, has at the time t a morally relevant desire that x, iff
a) A desires or likes that x at t;
b) a benevolent keeper of A who is fully informed and only thinks of the interests of A would satisfy the desire or like;
c) the desire (like) is not the effect of drugs;
d) A is not trained to desire or like x in a way that could be changed by new training.

There are cases of brain damages of human beings and severe handicaps that make the idea of increased knowledge and experience nonsense. A human being can be in a state where she cannot experience, remember or compare experiences. In such cases her desires and likes – if she has any – must be rather inadequate, and reasonable hypotheses about what she would like must replace her expressed desires. In such cases too the benevolent keeper takes over.

This limitation of the class of morally relevant desires is justified by three different reasons: first I believe that these are the desires we want satisfied for ourselves. We believe that our desires are well-founded in this way, that's why we try to satisfy them. As soon as we become convinced that they will change with more information or experience and this new knowledge is not only theoretical, they will in most cases change. Secondly, there are two ways of maximizing satisfaction and minimizing dissatisfaction: by satisfying the desires or by changing them. But when these desires are concerned the second possibility is not actualized. Thirdly I believe that behind these two arguments lurks a third which is connected with the idea of human autonomy. To grant well-informed desires a central place in ethics is to respect a person's autonomy. As a matter of fact this might be the most important argument – to take the unchangeable desires of a person seriously is to let him decide for himself. Thus the moral core of such an ethics will be respect rather than value maximization. This respect also explains the prime importance of second order desires, which express the person's own choice to a higher degree than mere whims and impulses. It furthermore explains the importance of need-satisfaction as satisfying someone's needs is to safeguard his possibilities to live his own life. Providing the prerequisites for a good life is more important than actually contributing to making life good, since it embodies the respect for autonomous persons to live their own lives. (Of course we also want our own autonomy respected, and so the argument can be made to go round in a narrow circle; but the circle is too narrow, so it is useless as an argument.)

Problems

But even if we accept that Richard Brandt is right in stating that the question of what has intrinsic value for all practical purposes can be replaced by the question of which desires would persist if this man were fully informed, we still have some problems to discuss.

First we have the problem of measurement. How do we measure the degree of satisfaction of desire? The most reasonable solution to the problem of measurement seems to be to let people make preference orders of possible worlds. Thus the object of desire is to be big wholes rather than separate desires for particular things or states. When we desire particular things they are usually parts of a greater context. I want to have new binoculars, because I want to use them when sailing. If I didn't have a boat, I wouldn't want them.

I believe that James Griffin is on the right track, when he maintains that we cannot in a simple way just add the values of separate satisfactions to get a sum which represents the total value of someone's life:

> We can never reach final assessment of ways of life by totting up lots of small, short-term utilities. (Griffin 1986, 34)
> ...the model for our final authoritative calculation / . . . / has to take a global form: this way of living, all in all is better than that. (*Ibid.* 34-35)[3]

On the other hand Derek Parfit (1984, 341) argues that the idea of personal identity which he believes is the correct one, "the Reductionist View", gives a reason to focus our interest on separate experiences and try to bring about as large a sum as possible of positive experiences (when the negative ones have been subtracted). (More about other ideas that the Reductionist View gives arguments in favour of utilitarianism below, pp 127-130.) But even if we accept the idea that life is more discontinuous than we used to believe, it does not follow that the value of even a short part of a life is a simple function of adding the value of the separate elements of this part. Combinations of satisfactions and dissatisfactions add to or subtract from each other in more complicated

---

[3] Also cf C.I. Lewis 1950, 488-495.

ways.[4]

The value of a part of a life is not just a result of the value of the elements making it up, but depends on how they are combined. G E Moore develops similar ideas in his concept of "organic wholes". Griffin uses a metaphor to express the same thought: "To some degree, estimating the values of these different ends is like determining the value of ingredients in cooking." (Griffin 1986, 35f)

A further problem connected with the idea of ascribing moral relevance to satisfaction of desire is the fact that desires change over time. Ought we to pay moral attention to the desire of the small boy to become a policeman, when growing old he no longer wants the same thing. The general solution to this problem seems to be that desires that get replaced by new ones have no force at all. The same is true of desires that just fade away (indifference in this case is taken as a kind of relevant attitude). There is no point in satisfying a desire that no one has.

Is the same true of desires about things happening after your death? I am not quite sure what to say: on the one hand you could say that your desires cannot change when you are dead, and therefore we ought to satisfy the desires expressed in last wills and so forth. On the other hand you could reason that the dead person does not want anything any longer, and nothing can be better or worse to her. While she lived she wanted strongly that certain things should happen after her death. She might have wanted to be certain that they were going to happen. This gives a reason for usually complying with last wills, although the reason then is that the living persons want to be sure that some of their decisions will be complied with after their death, and they could not be certain unless we generally complied with people's last wills. But this

---

[4] Karl Duncker has – in connection with pleasures – made the observation that if you eat candies while listening to the *marche funebre* in the seventh symphony by Beethoven, the two experiences do not interact, you experience them so to speak separately and must focus your attention on the different experiences in turn; but listening to less solemn music can be combined with the eating of candies: then the two experiences strengthen each other and will form an integrated and heightened pleasure. Even though this special example may not be universal but express certain idiosyncratic feelings of Duncker's or is a result of his education, I believe that there is something true in this observation: the value of parts of life is not just a sum of the value of their constituent parts – the combination is important too. (See Karl Duncker 1940.)

does not give us a reason to comply with someone's last will, when we could do something else secretly and no one would ever get to know it. This points to a more general problem, which is whether it can really be true that unknown satisfaction of desire matters. Can a man's life be better or worse as a result of something that he does not know of? An example borrowed from Dan Egonson will highlight the point:

> A person A is extremely jealous and therefore intensely wants his wife to be faithful to him. Suppose that a friend B, is aware of A's predicament but thinks it is ridiculous and wants to play A a joke. He then tells A in apparent confidence a false story about A's wife and the man C next door. B finds A's desperate reactions to this so funny that he continues to keep him in the misconception. (Egonsson 1990, 36)

Now it seems very queer to say that this man's life is not worsened by this false information, although as a matter of fact his desire – that his wife be faithful – is satisfied. Egonsson tries to save the idea that satisfaction of desire and nothing else is what matters morally by using the argument that we usually want to have true information, not to feel dissatisfied and so forth. Therefore, not all of A's desires are satisfied in the situation described. But the argument is weak and A's life is very much worse than if he had got some false information on some trivial matter. So you cannot save the theory by the idea that the sad problem for A is the fact that his desire for truth has been frustrated. On the other hand it seems to me that Othello would have been worse off had Desdemona in fact betrayed him, without him ever coming to know it, than he is in falsely believing that Desdemona is unfaithful.

Othello is utterly desperate because he believes something to be true, which he fears. He believes that the woman he loves has betrayed him. If he could be convinced that his suspicion is unfounded he would be happy again. Thus his desperation is a reaction to a situation he (falsely) believes to be a fact. The confirmed hedonist would say that the desperation is what makes the situation bad. Therefore a situation where Desdemona in fact betrays Othello but he never comes to know it rates – as far as Othello's life is concerned – equal in value with the situation where Desdemona is faithful and Othello knows it. This I cannot believe.

But Othello's situation as described by Shakespeare is bad, nonetheless. How can this be explained in terms of frustration of desires? After all Othello's desire that Desdemona be faithful to him *is* satisfied. I believe that we must say that he also wants to be certain that

Desdemona is faithful. And it is this desire which is frustrated. This is not just a general wish for true information, but a desire to be firmly convinced of facts that matter very much to him. I believe that we are, at least sometimes, more interested that certain propositions really are true than that we know them to be true (or believe them to be true). And if such desires were to determine our own actions they ought also to decide what it is right or wrong to do to others. I therefore conclude that unknown satisfaction can be of moral relevance. If so, it might even be the case that the wants of dead persons are morally relevant. However, I find the problem of the desires of the dead more problematic, since if the dead person no longer exists, there is no one who can be satisfied. And it seems to me that the moral force of desires depends on the fact that there *is* someone whose desires can be satisfied or frustrated. This is contrary to the opinion of Egonsson who takes the wants of long since deceased persons to be of equal moral relevance as the desires of those living now or in the future. When it comes to the desires of those living in the future I believe that we ought to take them into consideration, granted that these future individuals *will* exist. If they are just possible people I will not count their desires.

But should we let well-informed desires – first or second order – play such an important role? Consider the following example (proposed by Torbjörn Tännsjö in 1990 II, 118ff): a person with compulsive behaviour is incapable of travelling by the underground or taking the bus. Therefore she cannot go and see her children and grandchildren, she cannot work and is unable to meet her friends. However, she is very sceptical about drugs and medical treatment. She is convinced that psychological changes ought to take place by gradual development and through deepened insight. A friend of hers, a doctor, has found a certain new drug very effective in cases of phobia, a pill which has immediate effect and no secondary effects. The neurotic does not, however, want to take the drug, neither does she want to be duped into taking the drug. Her friend, however, puts the drug into a glass of brandy which she offers her without telling her that the drug is in it. The former neurotic suddenly finds that her horror of travelling by bus or underground has disappeared. She starts living a normal life and is happy and grateful to her friend for giving her the drug. Didn't the doctor act rightly?

On the one hand you could say that since the neurotic is happy *now* and does not want her old phobias back, the action was justified. But on the other hand, can the desires *after* the treatment be the ones that count? Suppose another person gives someone else a pill that makes him a happy slave. After taking the pill he wants nothing else but to be a slave. Or to take a more realistic example when you give a person crack and from that moment this person wants nothing else but get another high on crack.

So it cannot always be true that what is important are the desires after the change, irrespective of how the change is carried through. You might argue that if the neurotic in the former example had really known the effects of the drug, she would have wanted the drug, but this desire is not actual so it does not meet my requirements. I believe that we have to respect her desires until we are able to change them by more information.

Further problems: morally suspect desires

Sadistic desires, lust for power, envy, malevolence, vindictiveness, and so forth might be attitudes difficult to change, but can they really be morally relevant in the sense that they give rise to *prima facie* obligations that they should be satisfied?

I will not on moral grounds exclude any desires from the class of desires that give rise to a supposition that they ought to be satisfied, since if I did, I must have some criterion of moral acceptability, and I will take desires and needs as the ultimate facts on which to base ethics. It is of course usually true that you ought not to satisfy the desires of the sadist or the rapist, but the reason is that they come into conflict with the desires of the victims, and these interests tend to outweigh the first.

It might seem as if this standpoint would come into conflict with the idea that the condition of well-informedness includes all kinds of knowledge, even moral knowledge. Would not morally suspect desires vanish if a person came to believe all relevant moral truths?[1] Well, *if*

---

[1] Jan Österberg has proposed the following way of reasoning: to prefer *a* to -*a* intrinsically is to believe that *a* is better than -*a*. Now the sadist's preference for someone's pain involves his belief that pain is better than pleasure, which it is not. Therefore true information would change the sadist's preferences. But this presupposes that an attitude is a belief about value – in a way it is; but the other way round: a belief about value is just an attitude. This is the reason why emotivists and prescriptivists deny that evaluations have truth-values. A naturalist of the subjectivist kind regards evaluations as, if not attitudes, at least statements about attitudes. Thus the sadist can only come to know something about his own preferences, and if he really likes someone to

they do, they are disqualified. The problem is what if they do not vanish – are we really to reckon their satisfaction as intrinsically valuable?

If there are no moral truths, moral knowledge is not possible and hence increased moral knowledge can change no desires. (Of course my idea about the moral relevance of desires in that case is not true either – it will have to be taken as a proposal to share these attitudes with me.) But if there are moral truths, there are two possibilities – either I am wrong, i.e. something other than satisfaction of well-informed desires has intrinsic value, or I am right. If I am wrong the important thing is what really has intrinsic value, you need not bother about criteria of morally relevant desires.

But suppose that I am right, then one of the moral truths is that satisfaction of desire is what matters morally. Can the coming to know that this is true, change my desires? I believe it can. Hitherto I might have striven for x, although I don't really want it in itself, just because I believed that x has intrinsic value. My new insight might change my desires, so that I try to consider what I really want. This does not seem problematic. But among the moral truths might also be some norms about what we ought to do to other individuals, e.g. that you ought not to inflict pain upon someone who does not want it. Such knowledge might change the desires of a sadist. But it is not certain that it will: the sadist might still desire the suffering of other individuals, although he understands that it is wrong to satisfy such desires. If so the desires of the sadist have some moral relevance, although you have to weigh this against the desires of others. This means that it will be difficult to satisfy them without mistreating others. The well-informed sadist will know that his desires are relevant but that it is usually wrong to satisfy them.

If we totally disregard the consequences for other individuals, or if these consequences are positive, it seems difficult to deny that the satisfaction of malevolent or sadistic desires would be valuable. Consider the situation in which a man is locked up in an asylum after committing sexual violence. He is well locked in and will never get out. As a matter of fact he will never hurt anyone more. Now you are going to visit the man, and he wants you to bring him the complete works of the Marquis de Sade and the latest report of Amnesty. Is it really a moral obligation to bring him some novels by Dickens instead? It seems to me that you ought to comply with his request, provided that you are certain that there is no probability that any treatment would relieve the man of his sadistic impulses, which might be better for

---

feel pain, it seems improbable that information would change this fact.

himself and the rest of mankind. But if this is impossible – ought you not to try to satisfy these perverse lusts of his?

Thus I cannot find any conclusive arguments against maintaining that satisfaction of any desires fulfilling the conditions in this chapter, is what ultimately matters morally. Nonetheless I believe that there is a class of interests that are even more important from the moral point of view. In the next chapter I will try to make clear how we should draw a boundary between this category of morally relevant desires and the more important interests, "needs".

Chapter 5

Needs

In the first chapter I stated that an individual has an interest in those things she desires and in the necessary means to obtain these. In the fourth chapter I discussed the first type of interests: what kinds of attitudes are morally relevant? Now I want to discuss the second kind of interests. In a wide sense we need all that is necessary to satisfy our desires. Therefore I will call these interests "needs".

I have already (in Ch. 1) hinted at the results of this chapter, I used "needs" to refer to necessary and in the situation sufficient conditions for a minimally acceptable life. In this chapter this concept is not presupposed – it is rather the result of the analysis.

There are two concepts which both can be expressed by the term "need" – one referring to certain psychological drives and one referring to certain causal connections between states. The first sense was discussed in the beginning of Ch. 3. This chapter analyses the second sense of "need". I first make some comments upon the use of "need" in the English language (which I believe hold also for some other European languages and also for some non-European languages which I have tried to check: cf Ch. 3, p 43).

"Need" in this sense thus refers to a causal relation between some states. This meaning (or near-related ones) of the word "need" has often been discussed in analytical philosophy: Paul Taylor 1959, David Braybrooke 1968 and 1987, A.R. White 1975, and Garrett Thomson 1987 among others analyse "needs" as necessary conditions for some goal.[1]

---

[1] Similar points can be made about related words in other languages as "Bedürfnis", "besoin", and "behov". Also in non-european languages like

Garrett Thomson 1987 gives the following scheme for interpreting all statements about needs:

A needs X in order for A to Φ in circumstances C if and only if X is a necessary condition of A's Φ-ing in circumstances C. (Thomson 1987, 3)

Thomson does not seem willing to accept that "need" can be used with a motivational psychological sense somewhat akin to "desire" or "want". But it is not uncommon to see "need" used interchangeably with "strong desire" for instance.[2] Therefore it is important to distinguish clearly between the two concepts that can be expressed by the same word "need". Someone can have a need in the sense of necessary condition without feeling a drive or showing a relevant behaviour tendency and *vice versa*. You can have a need for a certain vitamin without feeling any special hunger for food rich in that vitamin. Rats have had their brains operated so that their want to sleep has disappeared; they stayed awake until at last they died from lack of sleep. You can feel an irresistible drive for alcohol without having a need for it. Lack of need satisfaction furthermore can have effects on the lives of plants and animals while not at all influencing their behaviour.

That the two senses of "need" – "necessary condition for some goal" and "fundamental drive" – get mixed up is explained partly by two facts. There is often some physiological connection between needs and behaviour impulses and there must be a natural adjustment between desires and behaviour of animals on the one side and the necessary conditions for their survival on the other. Animals whose desires and needs are not correlated will usually not live long enough to beget offspring. This adjustment will obtain in the natural environment of the animal, which explains why rats eagerly consume saccharin, which they do not need. In their natural environment saccharin has not been generally available. Plants rich in sugar on the other hand have provided needed nourishment. Had both sugar and saccharin been generally available in the normal environment of rats, natural selection would have favoured those rats that could discriminate between the two and preferred sugar.[3]

Persian and Turkish there are equivalents. See some notes in Ch. 3.

[2] Cf Ch. 3 on psychological uses of "need".

[3] I have borrowed the idea from Kai Sørlander 1989, 25. Also cf J. Olds, "Physiological Mechanisms of Reward", *Nebraska Symposium on Motivation* 1955: "Needs do not really enter in the control of

A third cause of confusion is that a good reason to desire something is that you need it. If you get convinced that you will not survive without x, then you have a rational reason to desire it. And such an insight can of course give rise to a desire.
   Nonetheless it is important to keep 'desire' and 'need' apart. You can have a need without the corresponding desire and *vice versa*. The concept of need to be analysed here refers to a causal relation between the one having the need, the circumstances in which she needs it, and a goal: what is needed is a necessary and in the situation sufficient condition for attaining some goal:

   A has a need for x in the situation s, if and only if, there is a goal y for A and x is a necessary and in s sufficient condition for A to reach y.

Here I diverge from most authors who have defined 'needs' in terms of conditions for some goal. The term is usually defined in terms of necessary conditions for some goal only. My reason for introducing the element of "in the situation sufficient condition" is that we usually have needs for a lot of different things, like oxygen, water, food, etc. And we need all of them. A person needs food *and* water – she will not survive without them. We *can* of course say that she has a need for water and a need for food, but if she cannot get water, her need for food is of no importance. It seems to me odd to maintain that she still has a need for food, even though this will not help her survive. When she is dying for thirst, she does not need food any more. (Cf pp 101f and 137.) I now want to clarify this concept of 'need' and delimit a certain class of such needs that are of special moral importance, *viz* 'basic needs'.

What has needs?

Practically any kind of entity can be the subject of a statement about needs. "The army needs more money." – "Plants have a need for light." – "The theory needs sharpening." – "The car needs repairing." All types of formulations of statements about needs might not be equally natural when stated of certain kinds of entities. That something needs something else can be said of almost anything. But to say that a non-living object has a need for something is a less natural expression. There are some differences of nuance, which depend on the fact that "a need" but not the verb "to need" seems to be connected with goals,

---

behaviour, except in the long run through the mediation of natural selection." Quoted from Peters 1958, 129.

desires, wants, etc, which we suppose that only living beings can have. But it is possible to use the construction with the verb "need" about all kinds of objects. I have chosen to define "a need" in terms of necessary an sufficient conditions for a goal because I am interested in a normatively interesting concept of 'need', a concept connected with living beings and their interests. But there are certainly other uses, which will not be touched upon here.

What is needed?

The usual way of expressing that someone has a need is to say that she needs some *thing*. Usually, however, some state or action is presumed; strictly speaking you do not need food or water, you need to *eat* food and *drink* water. More strictly even, what is needed is getting nourishment which you can get by eating food or by getting nourishment injected in your veins or in some other way. What is to be done with the thing needed can be self-evident in the case of food. But if Peterson needs a car, it is not quite obvious if he needs to own one; he might need to borrow one, to drive one, to have access to a car or something else. Often some vague and ambiguous verb is presupposed like "have", which in connection with certain objects like cars or wells can have some more or less juridical sense, but which connected with other goods like oxygen or love, does not have a juridical or semi-juridical meaning. Often one would gain in clarity if one specified the need-relation between A and *x* by explicitly stating what A needs to do with *x* in order to realize *y*. "Need" can be used as a modal verb like the Swedish counterpart "behöva". Alan White (1975) analyses "need" mainly as a modal verb and therefore also points out the need to construct what is needed as a complete phrase consisting of verb and object.

Need-statements with no mention of goal are elliptical

When talking about needs you sometimes don't mention a goal. This does not mean that some needs are not related to goals. It just means that the goal is sometimes taken for granted. It has been maintained, however, that there are two kinds of need statements: you can either talk about needs in an instrumental sense or in an absolute or categorical sense. This or similar distinctions are made by among others Kai Nielsen (1963 and 1969), David Miller (1976), Georg Henrik von

Wright (1982), David Wiggins (1985), David Braybrooke (1987), and Garrett Thomson (1987). Only when using "need" in its instrumental sense, it is reasonable to say that the statement is elliptical, if you leave the goal out, according to this view. If used in an absolute sense the statement is not elliptical, although no goal is mentioned for which the satisfaction of the need is a necessary condition.

But to me it seems evident that if 'need' is analysed in terms of necessary (and/or sufficient) conditions, it is always adequate to ask "necessary for what?" Alan White (1975), Anthony Flew (1977), and others agree in this. The distinction that von Wright, Wiggins, Braybrooke, Thomson, and the rest in that camp, want to emphasize is that between necessary conditions for arbitrarily chosen goals and some goal which can be taken as given and presupposed by certain statements about fundamental needs.

Is there any given goal for human beings or living beings in general, a goal so commonly acknowledged that it is reasonable to take this goal as presupposed by all categorical need statements? Even if there were such a goal – survival for instance – it seems correct to say that the statement that A needs x is elliptical unless completed to the full statement that A needs x in order to survive. But it seems necessary to distinguish, at least in some way, this use of "need" from other uses like A needs a car to get to his summer cottage in a convenient way, or that A needs a boat, if he likes fishing. From now on I will use the term "basic needs" to refer to conditions that are necessary and sufficient for a goal, which can be presupposed as a goal for all human beings or all animals. In the last four sections before the summary of this chapter I will state in more detail what this goal is. Since the rest of this essay will be dedicated to analysing the concept of 'basic needs' and its place in normative contexts, I will however for the sake of brevity often just write "needs" and take it to refer to basic needs, if I do not explicitly state that I refer to other senses of "needs". This of course does not mean that my use is not elliptical: on the contrary my use of "needs" while leaving the goal out is clearly elliptical for "A has in s a need for x in order to obtain the goal y" (y is to be specified later).

It can further be noted that the kind of goal presupposed by statements about needs seems to be something which the individual who has the need must be a part of. You can certainly have as one of your most important goals that peace and justice should prevail in South Africa, but unless you yourself are supposed to live in this new South Africa, you cannot have a need for the conditions necessary for realizing that goal. The goal presupposed by a need statement (or spelled out in it) must be some goal which you participate in. This seems to be so by virtue of general habits of language use. But it also seems to have some normative import. In Ch. 6 I will defend a principle of right to need-satisfaction, and it seems as if you have rights to things that have a direct bearing on your own life. (Cf also the discussion of self-related desires in Ch. 4.)

Needs are not just acute lacks

Some needs are continuous, they must be satisfied at comparatively short intervals, if the goal is to be realized. This is the case for instance with the human need for oxygen. Other needs arise at a certain point of time, and lack of satisfaction has longer or shorter effects. Lack of growth hormone during childhood results in dwarf-stature for the rest of the child's life.

Needs are in a way relative to circumstances

In the climate of Greenland human beings have needs for warm clothing to survive, in Central Africa this need is not so important. Old people have a need of more light than younger people in order to read the newspaper. Therefore you must take into consideration the circumstances under which there is a need. In my definition of "need" I have chosen to make that clear by making needs relative to a situation. The situation can be specified in different ways, so that it will be clear in which circumstances a certain need prevails. "Situation" is to be taken in a wide sense, so that illness for instance can characterize a situation so that a need exists when a person is ill but not otherwise. If I had diabetes I would have a need for a regular intake of insulin. Sex, age, and social roles also can be circumstances determining which needs I have. In a wider sense, needs of course vary with a lot of different circumstances. Systems of legal and social rules determine what you need in some contexts. To go abroad legally you need a passport for example.

Thus needs in general are relative to circumstances, society, historical epoch, etc. Basic needs are also relative to circumstances in a way. But on a very abstract level, they are not. We must therefore try to reach some conclusion on the relativity of needs.

One problem in this context is the following: can you need something that is not available? Could you for instance say that medieval man needed vaccination or that a short-sighted paleolithic hunter needed glasses or a laser operation? On the one hand it seems as if the need for vaccination was even greater during the Middle Ages if you were to survive the Black Death for instance, and that a short-sighted hunter dependent on catching his prey had an even greater need for a laser operation than modern man, who can use a lot of technical facilities to make life comfortable without ever hunting. But on the other hand it seems absurd to say that someone has a need for something that is not even in principle available at the time. Should we then conclude that HIV-infected people do not need an effective anti-aids medicine?

As I intend to tie needs to rights it seems reasonable not to include needs for the impossible among those needs on which rights are based, since I believe that there is some connection between 'ought' and 'can'. I will not claim that 'ought' straightforwardly implies 'can', since there are uses of "ought" which do not logically imply anything about possibilities. However, there seem to be some presuppositions tied to categorical ought-statements which make it odd to claim that you ought to do the impossible. Therefore needs in a normatively relevant sense cannot be for the impossible. What we can say about the HIV-infected persons is that they have a strong need that medicine against aids will be developed, unless this is impossible. But it is not reasonable to claim the need for vaccination against the Black Death on behalf of medieval man since the medical technology and knowledge of the human body and immune system at that time were so rudimentary that there was no reasonable hope that even the idea of vaccination could have occurred to the scientists of the time. Thus even the availability of certain commodities will enter into our considerations when we try to determine which concrete needs a certain individual in a specific situation has.

We must however be careful so that we do not accept as a fact that a person in Bangla Desh during a famine in the 20th century does not need food. It is in no way impossible to procure food for everybody now living on this planet. This means that my proposal that we should not say that someone needs x, unless x is available must be qualified. Should we run into a situation where the resources of the earth would not be sufficient to feed the entire population we are not to say that some lack the need for food, but that the scarcity makes satisfaction impossible. Simple scarcity is not enough to justify denial of needs. It is the technological or logical impossibility satisfying any need of a certain kind that makes talk of needs void. Technological impossibility is first and foremost to include empirical impossibility, that is the logical incompatibility between statements that satisfaction of the need in question is possible and true relevant laws of nature; but also included are the incompatibility between the technological level of a certain society and the availability of means of satisfaction. The technological level is then taken to be given and not easily changed within the foreseeable future. This means that technological and scientific breakthroughs can turn something into a need which hitherto has not been a need.

...but in another way they are not

Needs can be described in more or less abstract terms. The more concrete the needs we want to capture the more relative they will be. But I believe that the most basic needs will not be relative when considered sufficiently abstractly. However, you could ask if they will not be so abstract that what is left is the bare need to survive in an acceptable way (or, if that is impossible, to die). Nothing else can possibly be said about concrete needs which will not in some way make the needs relative to historical, social, and other variable circumstances.[4] You cannot even say that the need for nourishment and water is immune to variable social circumstances, since how much calories and water you need varies with your body size and during some periods of history people have been shorter than they generally are nowadays. This can in its turn be a function of how much nourishment you get during childhood, so there is a certain interdependence between needs and the possibility of satisfaction.

I propose the following solution to these problems. You have basic needs, characterized abstractly, for everything that is necessary and sufficient for a minimally acceptable survival, or, if you have no prospects that your life will ever be minimally acceptable again, you have a need for the means to get rid of your suffering – in the extreme case even to die. Which specific needs a certain individual will be ascribed is left for experts in medicine, biology, physiology and so on to determine. They then have to take into consideration the specific historical and social circumstances under which the individual lives. A point of departure should then be that circumstances that it is not possible for the individual to change will be taken to constitute objective constraints that determine which specific needs she has. Thus the trapeze artist's need for a safety net will not be considered a basic need, since this need is dependent upon the individual's choice of

---

[4] Cf the quotation from Marx on p 24.

occupation and not necessary to safeguard a minimally acceptable life. Borderline cases will be such circumstances which it is not possible for individuals to change in isolation, but which can be changed by collective action. Say for instance that to survive in a capitalist society you have to have a job with a salary. This you cannot change. However, under certain circumstances the working class could change the society so that this will not be necessary. Then you could say that as long as capitalism prevails you really do need a job with a salary. But assume that there is great unemployment and as a result many starve to death. You can then say that the unemployed (and perhaps the great mass of people) need a radical change of the society.

Basic needs must be satisfied

If there is a need, then there is a goal which will not be realized, unless the need is satisfied. The satisfaction is irreplaceable. David Wiggins (1985) has proposed that this irreplaceability is a question of degree. We must have protein, but meat and fish can be replaced by protein from soya beans. The more you have to lower the goal when you replace x, the thing needed, with something else, the more irreplaceable x is. If y is a minimally acceptable goal and x is necessary for the attainment of y, then x is necessary in a strong sense and the need for x is as strong as possible.

But my analysis differs from almost all others in that I require that what is needed must be both necessary and in the situation sufficient to reach the goal. My main argument for this is that if a certain means is necessary for a certain goal, but the individual nonetheless will not reach her goal, then the moral import of getting this means seems to dwindle. Since I want to state a moral principle to the effect that individuals have rights to need-satisfaction, it therefore seems better to require that "needs" be restricted to necessary *and* sufficient means. This might seem a merely verbal question, and it might even be unnatural linguistically speaking to require that the needed state is both necessary and sufficient in the situation. But it seems to me that if a person is lost in the desert with neither food nor water, he needs both. If a pilot can drop only food to this man, who nonetheless will die from lack of water, it is certainly true that he needs food, but this is morally speaking of no importance. Thus I want to restrict "basic needs" in the morally relevant sense to means that are both necessary and sufficient for some goal.

You might be tempted to point out that earlier (pp 53 and 67) I wrote that I do not want moral considerations smuggled into the definition of 'need', and wonder whether this is not an example of such a consideration. In a way it is a moral consideration; but it is not a consideration of the kind that I want to get rid of, namely such that requires a normative decision when deciding whether someone has a need or not. That is what I want to avoid.

In order not to include too much in the concept of "basic needs" the goal I have chosen is *a minimal level of well-being*, which now has to be specified.

...or else someone will suffer harm

There is a rather great consensus among those writing about the concept of 'basic needs', that unless they are satisfied for someone, she will suffer harm.[5] But "harm" can be used both to refer to the lowering of someone's welfare and to state that someone has suffered something intrinsically bad and presumably in several other ways. It is reasonable for instance to say that the owner of a factory suffers some harm from a strike (this at least must be the intention of the striking workers). Likewise a politician is harmed by the revelation that he has been bribed. Thus it can truly be maintained that owners of factories have a need for anti trade unionist laws, and that corrupt politicians need censorship. But these kinds of needs cannot be the kind of needs intended when we talk about *basic needs*. We have basic needs as human beings (or animals), but the needs of the capitalist and the corrupt politician are tied to their social roles and their satisfaction is not necessary in order to have a minimally acceptable life – therefore they are not basic.

Thus not every form of harm can be acknowledged as giving rise to basic needs. In the sequel I will discuss three kinds of harm which seem to me to be implied in everyday talk about basic needs and which at the same time explain the supreme moral standing of basic needs. These three forms of harm are death, suffering, and impediments to the development of essential human (animal) traits.

---

[5] See for instance: Miller 1976, von Wright 1982, Braybrooke 1987, and Thomson 1987.

Death

Most writers agree that among basic needs are at least those which it is necessary to satisfy to guarantee biological survival.[6] Even if survival were presupposed as the only goal related to basic needs, it is clear that there must be many basic needs common to all human beings (many of them common also to all higher mammals). In addition this way of delimiting basic needs will include the special needs of individuals with certain diseases and handicaps: the diabetic needs extra insulin and the haemophiliac extra blood.

It is important to note that the boundary between life and death nowadays is more wavering than it used to be. To be kept in permanent coma in a respirator can hardly be called a human life. If there were therapies that could bring someone out of such a state back to a conscious life, she would have a basic need for them, given that her conscious life would be acceptable and not only prolonged suffering.

The problems concerning the boundary between life and death are connected not only with medical progress, which makes it possible to keep some parts of the human body going while certain important functions are irreversibly lost, but also with the problems concerning what makes an individual *this particular* individual, i.e. what must be left in order to make true the proposition that *this* individual survives? Suppose that a person of the age of 30 is hurt in an accident, so that he is brought back to the level of a two-year-old child. Has this patient survived or not? Essential traits which characterized the 30-year-old person have disappeared. If you could restore his brain functions to the state before the accident, it would seem as if he had a need for such treatment. But if this is impossible, it seems more natural to say that we now are confronted with a new person (whose needs of course are also morally relevant, but may not be the same as those of the grown up).

These considerations point to the fact that the concept of 'death' ought to be tied to the individual concerned. A person can be considered dead when most of her brain functions have permanently ceased to function, *or* when they have changed so much that it is most natural to say that the former person has been replaced by someone else. Concrete problems in this context can be of the following kind. Suppose that we

---

[6] Usually this is mentioned just in order to take a step forward and in the next sentence add further needs. Cf e.g. Benn & Peters 1959; also cf Springborg 1981, 71.

find effective methods of curing schizophrenia. Would a person cured from his schizophrenia be the same person as before the treatment? Or suppose that some method is found to free a mongoloid of his extra chromosome, will a person cured of his mongolism be a different person or will he develop his "true self"? Such questions seem to presuppose an answer to the question about *who* a certain person really is. This means that we have to find a solution to the problems connected with 'personal identity', discussed since the time of Locke, but with no satisfactory solution in sight as yet. This is not the place, however, to solve these problems. Let us be content with stating that a person can be harmed either by being killed, *or* by being changed so much that she no longer is the same person. We can then leave it to further philosophical discussion to decide which changes are of that kind. But when the philosophical problems concerning death and identity are solved, it is a scientific task to answer the question of which needs must be satisfied to secure survival.

Furthermore there are certain conditions which must obtain if a human being is to live a minimally acceptable human life. Some of these are connected with the absence of suffering – life can be worse than to be unconscious or dead – and some are connected with ideas of what it is to have a *human* life, i.e. what is essential to be a human being. Some such conditions can no doubt be formulated concerning essential conditions for being an animal of a certain kind too, for instance to be able to fly if you are a bird (although not an ostrich, of course). These conditions are difficult to state clearly but are nonetheless essential or else we distort our moral experience (and our most central wants and desires).

Suffering

What is necessary for survival is thus needed. But it is not reasonable to delimit basic needs to such an extent. First of all there are states which are worse than to be dead, such as severe, uncompensated suffering without hope of recovering. We also have basic needs for what is necessary to escape such states. If those needs cannot be satisfied, we have a need to get rid of our suffering, even for the means to shorten our lives.

I propose that as a first approximation we should let subjective appraisements judge which these states are – a person, who prefers death to the life he looks forward to has a basic need for what would make his life worth living to himself. Many different things will be needed in this way, not only are there pains no one can endure, but in addition there are other forms of suffering. Someone cannot live without the love of a certain woman, another must have a yellow Skilling banco stamp, a third one will not survive the occupation of his country. So we must add some further conditions. First we should of course add those conditions on morally relevant attitudes discussed in Ch. 4. In this way we can eliminate sudden, irrational suicidal impulses caused by betrayed love and suchlike.

But there can still be left very special, idiosyncratic wishes to die, which do not seem reasonable to others. A person has collecting stamps as his most prominent interest. He seems to have a chance to get a yellow Skilling banco, but fails and takes his life. Do we have to accept that this man had a basic need for a yellow Skilling banco stamp? We can of course be sceptical about the assumptions in the case, for it is hard to believe that he would still have this desire if fully informed. He could change his project and begin collecting butterflies instead, or devote his life to science. But let us take for granted that his life will not be worth living to himself unless he gets his stamp. Must we accept that he then has a basic need for it? I would say that this person – and others similar to him – has a *personal project*, something that makes his life worth living to himself and without which it will be meaningless. Since such projects are not common to all and express personal choices, I will not take them to give rise to basic needs. It is true that the diabetic also has a need that is not common to all. But he has a goal – to survive – which is common to all. The philatelist on the other hand has in a way chosen his project. If he made an effort he could change it. He may not do so, he may not want to do so, but in a trivial sense it is possible for him to change it in a way that it is not possible for the diabetic to change his goal and his need for insulin. The sorrow of the philatelist, when he does not get his stamp, is of course not chosen, but his sorrow *depends* upon a personal choice of his. Perhaps "choice" suggests that a person can change his project whenever he makes an effort to do so (Jean-Paul Sartre can be interpreted to maintain such a view of human freedom in 1943). The presupposition behind drawing the line between basic needs and necessary means for personal projects here, is that persons really have in their power to change their projects. If this is not the case, the line should be drawn somewhere else. Thus with this reservation I will count only those needs that are common to us all, and those needs that cannot be changed, since they are related to those goals that we all have and hardly can change, as basic needs.

First we have the needs for such things as are necessary and sufficient to avoid grave illness and handicap. Some vitamins and hormones are for instance essential if we are to stay healthy. Of course there are trivial diseases like colds and ingrown nails which we can endure without feeling that our lives are not worth living. So I think that we ought to delimit the class of illnesses and handicaps which we have basic needs in relation to, to grave illnesses which threaten our life or which mean severe suffering. Some minimal level of normal functioning must also be presupposed. Where to draw the boundary is not altogether clear: we are told that Brentano thought it was a gain to become blind, since he then acquired a greater ability to concentrate on philosophical problems. But in the normal case I believe that blindness is the kind of handicap we want to avoid, even if it does not make our life so bad that it is not worth living.

I want to stress that I am not saying that the life of a blind man is worse than to be dead, so that all blind persons need active euthanasia. It seems more reasonable to maintain that there are certain basic needs which it is necessary to satisfy if we are to survive without unbearable suffering. To these basic needs are added those needs that it is necessary to satisfy in order to keep the ordinary function of vital organs going. We have basic needs for the necessary means of keeping our body functioning. But it is not always necessary to satisfy these needs to guarantee a *minimally* acceptable life. Thus there are two categories of basic needs, one of which is more important than the other. This means that there is so to say some distance between the minimally acceptable life in the strong sense and the level where all basic needs are met. This seems to be in accordance with our common sense opinion that some basic needs can be left unsatisfied: it is tragic but it does not make life unbearable to lose a limb or lose one's sight. There is therefore a difference in importance even among basic needs.

There is of course no clear-cut borderline between these two kinds of needs or these two levels of existing, but I will nonetheless distinguish between a '*minimally acceptable life*' and an '*acceptable life*', where it is necessary to satisfy all basic needs in the strong sense in order to reach the first level, and all basic needs – including those related to normal functioning of bodily organs and normal circumstances of a human life – if we are to reach the second one.

But must we avoid all suffering that is so severe that we would prefer to be dead (or unconscious)? A great deal of such suffering is common to all mankind (and in many cases to all higher mammals), but some of them are tied to our personal projects and strivings. Let us first take a look at those sufferings that are common to us all, and consider the more idiosyncratic forms of suffering later on.

In traditional axiological literature pain is often considered the paradigm of such suffering. However, there are trivial pain sensations which are hardly incompatible with an acceptable life, indeed hardly incompatible with a good life: your child pulling your hair, or you feeling pain and exhaustion at the end of a football match, for instance, are pains which are natural parts of a good life. Furthermore even very intense pain sensations are bearable if they are short and you know that they are. But pains that are so intense that you cannot concentrate on anything else – work or pleasure, e.g. – belong to the category of appalling pains, they are intrinsically undesirable.

In the category of suffering can also be included other strong unpleasant sensations, such as electric shocks, intense itching, nausea, strong cold or heat, unpleasant smells and others. In all these cases we must say that at least unpleasant sensations that are so strong that they prevent our concentrating on anything else are such that it is reasonable to suppose that most people would prefer to be unconscious rather than experience them, unless the experience is instrumentally valuable in some way. Whether or not we would experience a certain pain or other unpleasant sensations as so disturbing that we would prefer unconsciousness, of course greatly depends on other circumstances. If we are absorbed by some interesting piece of work, or if we are deeply in love, the pain or the sensation must be stronger if it is to be experienced as unbearable, than if we are occupied by trivial pursuits. But I believe that what matters morally in the last analysis are rather complex wholes, parts of lives or something like that. In a life (or a part of a life) some suffering can be compensated for; it is the uncompensated suffering that makes life unbearable.

Not only unpleasant sensations of the kind roughly characterized here can be a threat to an acceptable life. Deep endocrine depressions, anxieties, phobias, and other moods of that kind are of course also abominable. If certain foods, chemicals, or some form of psychotherapy are necessary to get rid of or to prevent such states for someone, then she has of course a basic need of it. What was said about compensated and uncompensated suffering and the degree of suffering, applies of course also, *mutatis mutandis*, to these moods.

More problematic are depressions and intentional sorrow, anxiety, horror, etc, which are caused by and intentionally directed towards external events – that your children die, that the world is unjust, that you know that you will die. If a pill was invented which made us euphoric at the death of our children, gay at the thought of our final departure, and happy at the grave injustices of the world, it does not seem a moral requirement that we distribute and make people consume it in the relevant circumstances. It is not only the belief that inadequate action would follow, but that it seems in a way valuable that you react in the "right" way in such situations. When your child dies it is suitable to feel sorrow. Pills that would diminish our natural reactions of sorrow and despair are not something we have a need for, except in extreme cases, where the sorrow will never leave us and prevents us from living our life and taking care of our surviving children and so forth.

There are pathological states where the horror would be natural if it had an objective ground: paranoia and certain phobias. There might be borderline cases between the true paranoiac and the man who feels "too strong" a fear of the atomic bomb. You may remember Yossarian in Joseph Heller's *Catch 22* who is convinced that someone wants to kill him; Clevinger denies this, but which one of them is crazy? However, it seems to me that clearly pathological cases of fear, anxiety, etc. ought to be treated by drugs or therapy, whichever way promises to be the most effective. Thus such mental illness gives rise to basic needs.

But the intentional sorrow, fear etc. is not incompatible with an acceptable human life. It is suitable to feel that way in certain situations: it is not the emotion but the situation that is bad. Then you could perhaps maintain that we have a basic need that the world affords us no occasion for such emotions. It does not seem reasonable to claim that the world ought to be such that we have nothing to grieve about, but it seems to be a reasonable moral obligation that we should try not to give our fellow human beings reason to feel fear, sorrow, or jealousy.

You could object that unhappiness is a state we want to avoid, and some forms of frustration of very deeply felt desires are what we find most abominable, in fact, they can make you feel that your life is not worth living. If suffering that is worse than being dead gives rise to basic needs when the cause is some malfunction of your glands, then why not accept that the philatelist has a basic need for his yellow Skilling Banco stamp? Would it not be more coherent to maintain that we need everything to be happy – or at least everything necessary so that our lives are worth living (to ourselves)?

If the diabetic has a need for extra insulin, which the normal human being does not have, why not allow the philatelist's desire to get a yellow Skilling Banco stamp to be called a need – after all he cannot live without it? Whether or not we should include needs derived from personal projects among basic needs is a terminological question. What is a substantial question however, is whether or not such needs give rise to moral claims. I will argue in the next chapter that they do in a way, but not the strict claims of a positive right to satisfaction as ordinary basic needs. As I said above there seems to be an important difference between the depression caused by not getting a certain stamp and the endocrine depression: the former depends on a choice of yours, while the latter does not. It is possible that we ought to distinguish in a similar way between intentional sorrow and depression caused by the failure of personal projects which we choose and such that are caused by features of the human nature, such as sorrow at the loss of one's children. It seems as if love for our children is not a freely chosen project: it is natural and unavoidable to feel sorrow when your child dies. Thus it might be reasonable to include such negative moods among those that give rise to basic needs – not however in the way that we ought to give drugs to people losing their children, but so that we must try to see to it that they don't lose their children if possible. However, there are difficult borderline cases, where the correct solution is not obvious.

Impediment of our natural development

Kaspar Hauser was locked up from his early childhood without contact with other people. His physical needs were satisfied, we may suppose. But he was not able to develop a human language or human contacts (until he was released from his prison). His development was stunted. Let us further assume that he suffered neither pain nor other unpleasant sensations, neither anxiety nor depression, neither illness nor physical handicap. His state nonetheless was such that we must say that he was afflicted by something intrinsically bad. His situation most probably caused him suffering, but let us assume that it did not. Wouldn't we nonetheless be prepared to call the impediment of his development something intrinsically bad with a similar justification as in the case of death: his imprisonment prevented him from almost all possibility of positively valued experiences and from becoming what he would naturally have been. His state was bad because of similar reasons as the brain-damaged 30-year-old person we discussed a few pages ago. Kaspar Hauser didn't change from a normal 20-year-old man – he was prevented from becoming one. His needs for freedom and human intercourse were frustrated and this stunted his development.

I think we can conclude that there are some fundamental conditions connected with being human which are not quite satisfactorily caught in the network of physiological needs it is necessary to satisfy if we are to survive without severe suffering. If you are never allowed to develop some specifically human features you are harmed as a human being. In a way such needs uniquely belong to human beings – but in another sense they do not: analogous reasoning can be applied for instance to keeping some animals in cages, I believe.

It is very difficult, however, to point out exactly which these needs are. But I think that we can learn from the story of Kaspar Hauser at least two lessons about human needs: people need some, however rudimentary, education, and they need a certain amount of freedom.That we need education is explained by the fact that human beings have very few (if any) instincts – complex patterns of behaviour conducive to the survival of the individual, the species, or the genes, which are triggered off by specific environmental *stimuli*. This means that we are uniquely adaptable among the animals now inhabiting earth, but at the same time that we have to learn almost everything we must do in order to survive. A human child cannot survive unless older people take care of it and teach it a a great deal – language, how to get food and shelter, and so forth. But of course, which kind of education is necessary, depends on which society you are going to live in. So the needs for education are in a very high degree relative to society.

That we need freedom is due to the close connection there is between the concepts of 'person', 'choice', and 'value'. Not to be free is to be prevented from doing what we want. If we are in all situations prevented from doing what we want, we therefore never realize anything valuable. But a benevolent, omniscient, and omnipotent dictator or keeper could anticipate every possible choice of mine and give me what I want without my own active efforts. I believe that in such a situation my capacity for choosing would successively wither, so that life would lose its meaning for me. Furthermore the idea of choosing and acting is an essential part of our concept of a person, and it is an important part of our conception of human beings that at least normal adult human beings are persons. Therefore some degree of freedom is necessary to live a human life.

In both cases – education and freedom – it is very difficult indeed to decide what degree it is necessary to safeguard. The problem is that when it comes to freedom and education my subjective view of value seems to break down, whether or not a certain individual feels a desire for freedom and education, he needs them both to be human, and it is good for a human being to be this. Thus you cannot use as a criterion of the necessary amount of freedom and education that an individual wants it in order to make life acceptable. This is true also of other basic needs, but the problem is that the suffering which decides what is to be counted as a need is in a way decided by subjective criteria. This is not possible when freedom and education are concerned.

One of the reasons behind ascribing moral relevance to desires is that you ought to respect other persons and their autonomy. But to be autonomous you must have some freedom and some education. Thus these are necessary to become and continue to be an autonomous person. Therefore human beings have needs for these things in the same way that we need some vitamins, whether or not we desire them.

This importance of human autonomy was also used to explain why we are to pay greater attention to the considered desires and the second order desires of persons rather than their more unconsidered desires (cf Ch. 4). Furthermore the respect for autonomous persons explains why the prerequisites of a good human life are more important morally speaking than the actual satisfaction of desires: to respect a person's autonomy we have to guarantee the necessary conditions for her to be able to strive and act as she herself wants to. Therefore the needs as delimited in this chapter are far more important than the satisfaction of desires.

This does not, however, solve the problem of knowing what degree of freedom and education is necessary – it just rules out the subjective way of deciding the question. Furthermore it seems as if freedom at least is very difficult to measure, so that it might be impossible anyhow to determine degrees of freedom (cf Tännsjö 1985). Therefore this part must be left in an unfortunately imprecise shape. But in concrete laws and institutions there are ways of stating more exactly which the most pressing needs are by declaring some freedoms and some minimal education as rights. There is a certain amount of arbitrariness in such conventions, but behind such judgements there are sound conceptions of needs, and the best way to decide which they are might be discussions leading up to conventions about rights; thus in this case we must state the rights first and let the needs be known by implication instead of the reverse procedure.

Summary

> The individual B has a basic need for C-ing x in the situation s, if and only if C-ing x is necessary and sufficient for B in s to live an acceptable life,
> or – if there is no chance of attaining a minimally acceptable life – C-ing x is necessary and sufficient in s to bring B's suffering to an end.

"An acceptable life" means that B survives and that she is not permanently ill or handicapped in a serious way. And "a minimally acceptable life" means that her life is not so bad in terms of suffering or frustration that she would prefer being unconscious rather than to live it. Suffering in this context does not include intentional sorrow, fear, jealousy, etc, which are caused by and directed towards external circumstances and which depend upon personal choices in the sense explained above. If B is a normal human being, an acceptable life also presupposes some amount of freedom and education, the degree to be determined relative to society by rational and fully informed persons. If B is an animal, a small child or a seriously mentally retarded or demented (senile) person the judgement of the value of her life is left to the judgement of a benevolent, fully informed keeper. In that case freedom and education is adapted to the individual concerned, the idea being that a minimally acceptable life allows at least some development of the characteristic features of the being in question. Of course the clause about the necessity of freedom and education is not to be interpreted so that a human being incapable of learning anything or completely exempt of autonomy has a life not worth living. Such a being ought to get the necessary means for making her life at least minimally acceptable with reference to her capacities.

When there is no hope of living a minimally acceptable life, B has a basic need to obtain unconsciousness, and where there are no prospects of rendering her life minimally acceptable, she might even have a need to die.

In the most narrow sense of "basic needs" we thus have needs for that which is necessary and sufficient for survival without unbearable suffering. Many of these are needs we have in common with at least higher mammals. As members of a biological species we can furthermore be said to have needs for propagation. These needs however are hardly needs of the individual – giving life to offspring is not included in the goal of "minimally acceptable life". Therefore needs connected with propagation are not included among the basic needs of the individual (they are rather needs of the species, if continued existence can be taken as a "goal" of the species).

Basic needs in the strong sense constitute a group of interests more important than other interests, simply because it is necessary to satisfy them if we are to have a life that is better than being dead. And it is necessary to satisfy the basic needs in the wider sense if we are to live acceptable lives, as unless they are satisfied most desires cannot be satisfied. This explains the importance of these interests from the viewpoint of the individual. On the other hand a certain individual can have a very important personal project, which makes him take grave risks or sacrifice his own life and basic satisfaction of needs. And you cannot from the fact that needs are important for the individual conclude that we ought collectively to satisfy needs first: it might be possible that a lot of desire satisfaction can outweigh some frustration of needs. This gives us a reason for taking a closer look at the the moral system sketched in the first chapter, which claims that basic needs are always to be satisfied before other interests are satisfied.

Chapter 6

Rights

In the first chapter a principle of morality was sketched, the content of which was roughly that each person has a right to need-satisfaction and a right to strive to obtain her goals as long as this striving does not come into conflict with the equal or stronger interests of others. It was argued that such a principle could gain almost unanimous support, because we all have needs to satisfy and goals to strive for, and no one is strong enough to be able to reach her goals on her own. This of course does not mean that we never have a right to strive for satisfaction of desires which do come into conflict with the desires of others; our right to strive for our goals is undisputed as long as it does not conflict with the strivings of others; when our strivings get into conflict we must have principles for solving the conflicts.

Now this idea will be spelled out a little more. I will argue that the equal right to need-satisfaction and the equal right to strive for our goals are rights we have good reasons to try to get accepted. But I will also argue that they are rights which correspond to our moral "intuitions" – at least they correspond to mine, and I want you to ponder whether they do not correspond also to yours. If we have sound reasons to try to get my principle accepted *and* it furthermore corresponds to our moral intuitions, I claim that we have found a plausible explanation of the content of the intuitions. Thus we need no longer speculate about a realm of specific, non-natural "moral facts". Our moral intuitions (and partly our moral praxis) are explained as rules and principles which we have good reasons to try to get accepted, and which we have therefore tried to get accepted, but perhaps in a more or less confused form.

However, these meta-ethical convictions are not the main theme of this chapter. Here I will state, spell out, and defend some principles of moral rights and corresponding morally required actions. This I take to be the main core of morality.

That someone has a right is in this context to be interpreted as that she has a *legally or morally guaranteed status*. If my status as free in a certain realm is guaranteed, then some legal or moral norms make it obligatory that others refrain from stopping me, when I am acting in that realm. If my status is legally guaranteed, then the law ordains some sanctions against preventing me from making use of my sovereignty. If it is morally guaranteed, then the person who tries to stop me, acts wrongly. All kinds of rights can be considered guaranteed statuses. If I have some so called welfare rights, they can be interpreted in this way too: that I have a right to need-satisfaction thus means that I am guaranteed satisfaction of my needs, as far as this is humanly possible. There has been a lot of work done to make clear distinctions between different kinds of rights and to lay bare the logical relations between these.[1] But much of this need not bother us in this context.

Here it will be enough to state that the right to need-satisfaction is to be interpreted as a positive right as well as a negative one, i.e. we are morally required not only to respect other individuals' lives and their possibilities of getting basic need-satisfaction – if they cannot themselves satisfy their needs, we are morally required to help them, if we can.

The second right – to strive for satisfaction of desires – is not a positive right against everyone. Whether or not we have a moral obligation to help others to satisfy their desires, depends on the personal relations between us. When we are bound by personal ties to others our obligation to help them satisfy their desires is stronger – friendship and love consist in this mutual support and engagement. I cannot see, however, that this type of obligation is a strictly moral – i.e. social conventional – obligation; it seems rather to be some kind of freely imposed obligations by virtue of our personal relationship, or, more

---

[1] Wesley Hohfeld introduced (1923) a classification of rights in four main categories: Claims, Liberties, Powers, and Immunities. This classification of Hohfeld has been extended, made more precise, and the logical relations between different types of rights have been investigated by Stig Kanger in "Rättighetsbegreppet" ("The concept of a right", *Sju filosofiska studier tillägnade Anders Wedberg. (Seven philosophical studies in the honour of Anders Wedberg*, 1963). Stig and Helle Kanger have further developed the theory in "Rights and Parliamentarism", *Theoria*, 32, 1966. But I am neither interested in juridical rights nor in the more subtle differences between types of rights. I will just use two types of basic rights: negative and positive.

accurate, our relation consists in these obligations among other things. If a person is very egotistical or paternalistic towards his friends, he *can* be "morally" condemned, but more probably such a man will lose his friends. Therefore it seems partly to be rational self-love that exhorts us to be nice to our friends, partly it is just a fact that most of us love some persons and therefore try to satisfy their desires. But we have no right to claim satisfaction of our desires.

When it comes to desires of someone we love or someone we have promised to help, all other things being equal, it is more important to satisfy a strong desire than a weaker one, simply because this is the desire I would satisfy myself, if they were mine and came into conflict. Thus if someone ought to do to me what I want him to do, he should satisfy my strongest desire. This however is complicated by the fact that many individuals do not strive to reach their most important goals, or are irrational in some other ways. Thus for instance the neurotic in his behaviour shows that his strongest desire is to wash his hands. Now I believe that this kind of problem can be solved if we assume that the neurotic would rather want to satisfy other desires if he could – his neurosis makes it impossible for him to satisfy any other desires than the impulse to wash his hands. But if he had it in his power he would rather do other things. This is further strengthened by the assumption that we ought to pay greater attention to second order desires than to those of the first order.

The rights are motivated by the importance the satisfaction of needs and desires has for each of us. We should therefore try to keep the violations of rights as few as possible. Thus I do not take rights to be side-constraints of the kind proposed by Robert Nozick (1974). The important thing is not that you keep your hands clean, the important thing is that as few rights as possible are violated, if they are of equal importance. (Cf Regan, 1983, 305-312.)

This means that the rights in this principle are not interpreted as in a strong sense inviolable. But this does not mean that the rights are void in those situations where it is necessary to violate them in order to save others from the same or worse violations. On the contrary: we couldn't violate a right if it isn't there so to speak. A right is always a reason for action (or omission) although it can sometimes be overridden by stronger reasons, i.e. by other stronger rights. Thus the rights are taken to be *prima facie* rights. This does not mean that I give in to utilitarianism. Violations of rights are only allowed in order to avoid more or worse violations of rights. They are not allowed as means to realize as great a surplus of pleasure over unpleasure as possible, in order to defend the state, or something like that.

When I say that a right is a reason for action (or omission) this does not mean that I always have a subjective reason to comply with the right. Thus rights are some kind of "objective" reasons for acting. They do, however, tie in with our subjective reasons in the following way: we all have subjective reasons that these rights are respected as far as our own interests are concerned. To get such a system of rights going in a society they must be respected in most situations. Since I have an interest that the system be in force, indirectly I have some reason to comply with the rights of others, although this reason can be overridden by stronger subjective reasons in some situations. This does not of course mean that it is right for me to violate the right in such a situation. What is right and wrong is determined by the rules. If I violate a right I therefore act wrongly.

Needs are more important than desires for each individual, since nothing positively good can be realized unless her basic needs are satisfied. This however does not in itself establish the lexical ordering of the two rights, since it could be the case that the frustration of someone's needs could be traded off against the raising of the general level of satisfaction of desires for very many. But I will argue that this is not possible. So the principle is to be interpreted as establishing a lexical order between the two rights: need-satisfaction always takes precedence over desire-satisfaction. This is further strengthened by the different characters of the two rights: we are always bound to respect the right to need-satisfaction both negatively and positively. The right to strive for desire-satisfaction is only negative as a general moral rule. However, someone's right to strive for desire-satisfaction can conflict with some other's right to need-satisfaction. In that case the latter's right is the strongest one. We have as a general rule no obligation to help others realize their personal projects or satisfy their desires, unless bound to them by personal ties, promises, or explicit undertakings. If two rights to need-satisfaction come into conflict the most urgent need takes precedence; the urgency is to be determined by the necessity of the thing needed to obtain a minimally decent life or to avoid unbearable and uncompensated suffering. When the rights to need-satisfaction of several individuals conflict, we should try to minimize the amount of frustration of needs, as least as long as the needs are roughly of equal importance. When the needs are of different weight – as when something is necessary if someone is to be spared a long unbearable suffering, and some others need something to get a fully acceptable life, i.e. a basic need in the strong sense conflicts with some more ordinary needs – the most important basic need usually takes precedence, even if several other, less important needs be frustrated.

Mutatis mutandis the same can be said of the right to strive for satisfaction of one's desires: the stronger and more important (i.e. the more intimately connected with central goals of ours) a desire is, the stronger the connected right to strive for its satisfaction, even if it comes into conflict with the strivings of others. This general idea is, however, balanced against the possibility to add many weak desires to be traded off against one stronger desire. Let us assume for instance that I want to own a certain painting by Joachim de Patinir. My desire to be able to enjoy it every day is much stronger than the desires of the visitors to the National Gallery to be able to have a look at the same picture once in a while. The visitors to the National Gallery are so many, that their desires taken together outweigh my stronger desire to own the picture. This kind of adding satisfactions of desires to outweigh the frustration of one person's *need* is not allowed which is explained by the supreme importance of need-satisfaction to each individual: if her basic needs are not satisfied – at least if she is so totally frustrated that her life is no longer worth living or if she is killed – then her life is sacrificed to render the lives of others better, and this is not allowed by the principle sketched here.

The adding of satisfactions of desires to make a sum which can outbalance some other desire, is not, however, always an easy matter of calculation. Say for instance that one lethally ill cancer patient wants to be helped out into the park of the hospital the first warm day of spring to be able to listen to the singing of the birds one of the last times in her life. Let us assume that this desire comes into conflict with the desires of two nurses that they should be able to take a coffee-break. It seems reasonable to suppose that the desire of the patient is stronger and more central to making the last days of her life as pleasurable as possible and that therefore her desire ought to be satisfied even if you combine the two nurses' desires. There seems to be no simple way of calculating the solution to such conflicts, you have to consider each situation separately.

As was hinted earlier all kinds of desires are accorded moral relevance as long as they meet the requirements proposed in Ch. 4. That means that also desires concerning other people may have moral relevance. If, however, my desire concerning your life goes against your own, the situation is more complicated. In such cases the person's own desires concerning her own life take precedence when they conflict.

The arguments in favour of the principles

If a correct moral judgment is a judgement that is implied by moral principles which a great majority have sound reasons to try to get accepted as a device for solving conflicts of interest, as I argued in the first chapter, then a serious moral judgement in a way is a guess about which moral principles will be proposed by rational and fully informed persons. Does this seem implausible?

It almost certainly is not true that this is what most of us do believe that we mean when we state a moral judgement. But what do we believe? There are lots of proposals about what we really mean when we state a moral judgement. I cannot, however, see that these different opinions concerning what we mean have so much real import on the interesting questions of morals – the questions about validity of moral norms, the existence of moral facts, and so forth. Besides it seems to me that the best way to study what we really mean by moral statements would be some empirical investigations, which have not been carried through.[2]

What I am proposing is thus not an interpretation of moral statements. I propose that we take a look at morals as a social phenomenon, try to find out what its functions can be, and try to formulate a system of principles which would fulfil certain purposes that we do in fact have. If such a system were to correspond in a sufficient degree to our moral intuitions I believe that we have at the same time got the best explanation we can get of our moral intuitions and a method of validating moral judgements. If the system were not to accord with our most deeply rooted moral convictions, of course the problem remains of what these are all about.

The purpose I posit for ethics is the solving of conflicts of interests. This is a purpose we in fact have, since we must live together with others. To fulfil this purpose the system must be able to win the adherence from a great majority (cf Mackie 1977). Thus the principles it contains must be acceptable to most of us.

T.M. Scanlon (1982) has proposed that our fundamental moral motive is "the desire to be able to justify one's actions to others on

---

[2] Admittedly you would then have to make use of the subtle distinctions proposed in the meta-ethical debate. Furthermore you would have to use many different methods to be at all certain that you had a grasp of what "we" mean when uttering moral statements seriously. But in the end the question about what we mean by moral statements must be decided by empirical methods.

grounds that they could not reasonably reject". (Scanlon 1982, 116) But how are we to interpret Scanlon's proposal?

One first way of interpreting it would be that you can justify your action, a, if and only if you can show that it follows from a correct ethical theory together with a true description of the situation that you ought to do a, or that it is right to perform a. But this cannot be the interpretation intended by Scanlon (cf Scanlon 1982, 117f), since it would make the possibility of justification depend on what ethical theory you – and the person to whom the action is to be justified – accepted. To a utilitarian you can only justify your choice of action by making it plausible that your action maximizes happiness, for instance. Since Scanlon clearly considers his proposal as an alternative to the ways you can justify utilitarianism (Scanlon 1982, 116 and 119), we must look for some other interpretation.

A second possible interpretation could be that you can justify your action a to a person, P, if and only if P if fully informed would want a performed. But it could be the case that a was the right action to perform in this situation although it disfavoured P, so that it could not be justified to P in this way.

So the idea cannot be either that you must justify your action by deriving it from valid moral norms, nor that it should be acceptable from the self-interested point of view of everyone concerned. There must be some third interpretation. Let us consider two situations:
1) You try to convince a rich person that you ought to take some of his money to provide for the costs of the medical treatment of a seriously ill person, who cannot afford the costs herself.
2) You try to convince a seriously sick person, that she is to abstain from a certain necessary treatment at a hospital, because if she gets the treatment a rich man will have to abstain from some money to pay for the treatment.
Consider the first situation: if the rich man accepts Nozickian principles of justice for instance, we cannot convince him that we ought to take his money; neither can we convince him that it is in his own interest to abstain from the money. But we could perhaps justify our action in a different way: we ask the rich man if *he* would claim the money if he were in the position of the poor woman. The rich man must reasonably admit that he would want someone to pay for his treatment, if he were ill and poor. Thus in this way we can justify to the rich man that we take some of his money to use it for the recovery of the poor woman.

But we cannot expect to convince the poor woman in the second situation, that the rich man should keep his money and that she should abstain from the treatment in the same way. She might recognize that she too would be greedy if she were rich and would not willingly abstain from some of her money. But she knows what it means to be sick and poor, and if she could remember this, the loss of some money could be justified to her. Thus in both situations someone would reasonably be persuaded that the satisfaction of basic needs are more important than to keep one's money. Therefore one of the actions can be justified to them both, but not the other.

Interpreted in this way Scanlon's proposal is a version of Kant's idea about universalizability. Kant formulates his idea of universalizability as a necessary (and sufficient) condition of valid moral norms in two ways: first it seems to be just a formal requirement – which norms can consistently be universalized. But this weak idea about universalization is complemented by a more substantial one, stating that an action is right given that I can want this kind of action performed whatever my situation and circumstances. A rich man can of course want some Nozickian principle followed in all situations, but he must admit, that *if* he were poor and needy, he would not want it universally applied. (Kant, *Grundlegung*, 2 Aufl., 423-424) Thus we can derive the moral norm that we ought to help those in dire need, according to Kant.

Now it it might seem probable that everybody would claim that others should help them as much as possible also to realize their desired goals. But this is not the case, since if they were very deprived and could help those better off only by sacrificing their lives, they would not want to do so. Nor would they, if their only way to help others was to abstain from all satisfaction of their own desires.

But human nature and the human condition are alike in their fundamental aspects, so everyone must admit the importance of need-satisfaction. Therefore decreased satisfaction of desires above the level where life begins to be acceptable can be justified, if it is necessary to make life bearable to someone else. This can be justified to anyone who really tries to put himself in the situation of those in need. But the converse is not possible except by the help of some abstract principles like Nozickian rights, social-darwinism or utilitarianism. According to these principles an action can be justified morally, although it means that someone loses her life or is condemned to unbearable suffering, if it is necessary and sufficient to obtain a greater surplus of happiness, or for the progress of mankind, or out of respect for property rights. But such actions cannot be justified to anyone who is only asked to place himself in the shoes of another and try to imagine if he would keep to the claims made in consequence of these principles.

My interpretation of Scanlon thus boils down to an idea of morals as legitimate claims. The foundation and content of morals are concrete claims put forward by concrete individuals. Those claims are justified if they were to be recognized whatever our situation would be.[3]

This seems to me to be a fruitful view of validating moral principles. I will argue that the principles I propose will not be reasonably rejected because of the following reasons.

Let us first consider the method of validating moral principles with the aid of reasoning from a hypothetical "original position" as it is sketched by Rawls (1972). This is not the same idea as that of Scanlon, but I believe that there are some connections. If it could be shown that someone would have reasons to agree upon some principles in the original position, then in a way it has been shown that these principles could be justified to him, at least under special conditions. As philosophers have almost unanimously argued, rational persons in the original position would not choose a maximin-strategy as proposed by Rawls, since it is too pessimistic. They must be utterly risk-aversive to choose that strategy – and they are not, states Rawls. But they have good reasons to try to avoid the worst possible outcomes, if they are not pronounced gamblers, which they are not, according to Rawls. They would therefore try to get some guarantees against premature death, severe suffering, maiming and so forth. My principle of the priority of need-satisfaction safeguards against such outcomes.

To safeguard the satisfaction of needs is the prime interest of everyone, since without it she cannot realize any of her goals. Therefore she chooses a system which guarantees that as few basic needs as possible will be frustrated. Then her chance of getting her needs satisfied will be as great as possible. Therefore, behind the veil of ignorance, she ought rationally to choose the principle stating everyone's right to basic need-satisfaction as a first principle of morals, if she takes this to be a social device for solving conflicts of interest.

If she is not placed in Rawls' innocent state of ignorance, she still has some reasons to choose this principle as she cannot be sure that she will always be healthy, strong, and rich, even if this is the case just now. Even the richest and strongest human being is vulnerable and would need some guarantees for her personal safety. It might however be the case that she would like to have a principle stating only a negative right to basic need-satisfaction, i.e. she might trust her own strength and wealth to give her what she wants as long as no one threatens her life or physical security. Therefore it is not so certain that

---

[3] "The right-making force of a person's desires is specified by what may be called a conception of morally legitimate interests." (Scanlon 1982, 119)

she would accept a positive obligation to help others to satisfy their needs – if she accepted such an obligation her own level of desire-satisfaction might fall drastically.

Is it not enough to show that rational individuals behind a veil of ignorance have reasons to accept a proposed principle? It might be impossible to find a principle which it is rational to accept and live by for every individual of flesh and blood with her circumstances fully spelled out. And so it seems: no principle with stronger constraints on egotistical behaviour than ethical egoism will be rational, as long as "rational" is taken to imply maximizing one's own utility. Furthermore, why would an individual be bound by a principle or an obligation she has not accepted (provided we accept the contractualist's analysis of obligation as emanating from agreement)? How can we be bound by a mere hypothetical contract?

I want to argue something quite different from the idea that it is always rational for every individual to fulfil the obligations emanating from a hypothetical or real contract. Everyone has a reason to claim as a right that his needs be satisfied. Since one cannot be sure that one will always retain his health and wealth, everyone has a reason to claim need-satisfaction both as a negative and a positive right. If he didn't have to give anything in return, he would certainly claim (at least) this. Secondly no one can reasonably expect others to help him unless they believed that he would do the same to them in similar circumstances. Thirdly, in many situations a person does not gain himself by helping others satisfy their needs. In such situations he does not have an egotistical motive for doing this. But the needy would claim their right to need-satisfaction nonetheless. In such situations self-interest and morals are opposed to each other. Thus the moral force of right-claims does not emanate from an agreement, it emanates from the urgency of needs and our interest in being able to reach our goals. But the idea of a just solution of conflicts of interests is explained by our mutual interdependence. Just solutions are those that can be justified to others.

Why would people not claim more than my principles – maximal satisfaction of desires, for instance? The reason is that every stronger claim implies the risk that you lose everything. If everyone is guaranteed not the satisfaction of needs, but instead has a right to maximal satisfaction of desires, or there is a general requirement that the average desire satisfaction be as high as possible, then it is possible that someone has to be sacrificed in order to reach the higher general level of welfare. And the one to be sacrificed can be you. That you cannot reasonably accept, unless you are a very pronounced gambler.

The second part of the principle is the strongest one that could gain general support, I believe. I would like to get your help in realizing my goals and projects. But I would not like to be morally bound to help you realize yours. I believe that non-interference is the strongest principle we can all agree upon. When it comes to realizing those of our dreams we cannot realize on our own, we have to come to terms with some others: if you help me, I will help you, or if you help me I will pay you for this, etc. Therefore the philatelist mentioned in Ch. 3 cannot claim a positive right to the yellow Skilling banco stamp – this is just a personal project of his.

Now I have not tried to show in a rigorous way that these principles would be chosen by rational persons whether behind a veil of ignorance or not. This might be interesting, but I believe that a lot of that kind of reasoning gives a false impression of proof. None of the presuppositions or idealizations which are necessary to make the argument hold are uncontroversial, and if you change them, the outcome will differ too. However, more formally rigorous methods showing what would be chosen in certain specific situations could be interpreted as arguments in favour of the belief that certain principles will prevail in the long run, since people would become more well-informed and rational, and the differences between them would tend to cancel each other. I believe that the most we can hope for in this context is to make it seem plausible that some principles for solving conflicts of interest could gain more or less general support. And I do not believe that acceptance is unimportant. I want to test the possibility of viewing morals as an agreement on fundamental principles for solving conflicts of interest. If it can be made plausible that some principles have not only a good chance to win general support but also implications most of us would also consider morally acceptable, then we would have moved some way towards a reduction of moral theory to a theory of rational behaviour. In the last analysis I would rather it should be so that the correct ethical theory is the one accepted, than the one that *would be* accepted by rational persons in some very special situation. A moral statement would be acceptable iff accepted? Not quite. Rather I would say that a moral statement is true iff accepted when people have discussed it for a long time, have had enough time to experience the consequences of different systems in practice and so forth.

Now what remains to be discussed are some arguments for and against the proposed system of rights, which will not be arguments concerning the probable acceptance of the system. *If* the proposed principles do not seem morally acceptable for other reasons, then this tells against both the system as a moral system and the idea that a correct ethical system is a system which we would agree upon (at least if it is accepted that I have made probable that my principles would gain general support). First I will present four arguments in favour of the proposed principles of rights, and then discuss five arguments against them.

Intuitive moral arguments in favour of the principles

1. The principles proposed do not require maximization of desire-satisfaction, but rather maximal respect for rights. This means that the principles are individual-oriented rather than value-oriented, although the motivation behind the rights is that the rights safeguard things valuable to those having the rights. The importance of individuals is stressed in that the principles require that first of all, all individuals covered by the rights are to have acceptable lives. This means that no individual is to be sacrificed to the greater general good, sacrificed that is in the sense that she is killed or left to suffer a life that is not worth living. The rights take individuals seriously by requiring that each individual is first guaranteed a continued acceptable existence (or if that is impossible an acceptable death). The rights are furthermore conceived as claims put forward by existing individuals, rather than abstract claims in terms of morals or value. I believe that most people, when not too influenced by moral theory, conceive moral claims in this way: morality arises out of claims for help, claims for not being ill-treated, claims for respect. At least this is the way I conceive of morals.
2. Secondly the proposed principles mirror the fundamental importance to individuals of basic need-satisfaction. Theories not paying attention to the fact that interests differ in moral urgency distort moral experience. People suffering from utter deprivation certainly have greater moral claims upon us than do people living a good life.[4] This is something a utilitarian theory cannot explain in a satisfactory way. But the lexical ordering of the two rights of my principles makes it morally required to make sure that no one is in dire need first of all. This is in accordance with our moral intuitions. Although I will not lay too much burden of proof on intuitions, principles going too much against our intuitions must be considered carefully. On the other hand, *if* intuitions support principles established by other reasons this supports them further, not because intuitions are taken as observations of a moral reality, but because they can tell us something about our conception of morality.

---

[4] This has been pointed out by Karl Popper (1945, Ch. 5 note 6, Ch. 9 note 2) and Knut Erik Tranøy (1967) among many others.

3. Thirdly by stressing the moral importance of the prerequisites of good lives, the principles emphasize the importance of respect rather than maximization as the central moral obligation. Autonomous persons ought to be free to strive for their own goals as far as this does not interfere with the equal rights of others. But no one can realize any of her goals and strivings if any of her basic needs is frustrated. Therefore the principle requiring need-satisfaction as a right expresses the idea of respect for persons as autonomous agents.

4. The fourth argument has already been hinted at in the discussion of Rawls and Rescher (pp 61-64): what seems outrageously unjust is not so much great inequality, but the fact that such inequality can mean that one person suffers or dies, while others live in luxury. When our intuitions about injustice are critically examined I believe that this is what they boil down to. (Cf the discussion on justice in Ch. 3.) And my first principle safeguards against such outcomes. Thus it is in accordance with deeply entrenched intuitions about justice and injustice.

Moral arguments against the principles

1. A presupposition of theories of rights, of theories of just distribution and consequently of the proposed principles is that the distinction between persons is morally important. It does matter whether some good or bad happens to this or that individual. To consider questions of distribution intrinsically important is to take the distinction between individuals to be of crucial moral importance. Derek Parfit, however, has given an argument to the effect that distribution is not such an important question as we usually believe. We exaggerate the importance of the distinction between individuals, because we have a mistaken concept of personal identity, according to Parfit. If Parfit's argument were sound we would have a reason to be sceptical towards theories which emphasize the distinction between persons and the moral import of distribution between different individuals. We would have got a reason against some of the arguments which seem to tell most strongly against the utilitarian neglect of questions of distribution.

Parfit's argument is that personal identity is not a "deep further fact" in addition to psychological continuity and similarity (Parfit 1984, 199-347). What there "*is*" is a body and a bundle of mental states, more or less connected through memories, intentions, and similarities. Parfit compares personal identity with the identity of a nation. Both the person and the nation are made up of parts which can be replaced by other parts; the nation is nothing beyond its territory and its citizens;

the self is nothing beyond the stream of mental states. The question: "Would this being be me?" cannot always be given a definite answer. Since identity, the unity of the person over time, has shown to be chimerical – there is no substantial *self* identical with itself over time – the boundaries between different parts within a life will be more important, and the boundary between your life and mine will be less deep, according to Parfit. But I cannot see that the latter follows. Let us accept for the sake of discussion that what we usually take to be the life of the same person, as a matter of fact consists of several different parts which successively pass over into the next, and where it is not the same person living all parts of the life. If questions about just distribution do have any relevance, this idea of personal identity seems to indicate – as Parfit points out – that you ought to consider the distribution between different selves in the same series as well as between different individuals in the ordinary sense. But the argument gives us no reason to think that the limit between different persons is less deep than if some other idea of personal identity were true. But Parfit maintains that this is an implication of his theory:

> If some unity is less deep, so is the corresponding disunity. The fact that we live different lives is the fact that we are not the same person. If the fact of personal identity is less deep, so is the fact of non-identity. There are not two different facts here, one of which is less deep on the Reductionist View, while the other remains as deep. There is merely one fact, and this fact's denial. The separateness of persons is the denial that we are the same person. If the fact of personal identity is less deep, so is this fact's denial. (Parfit 1984, 339)

It seems to me as if there were *two* facts and that Parfit mixes them up. One thing – the true thing – is to say that it is not very dramatic to deny that we are the same person, if it is not certain that *"one"* person is the same person all the time. To deny that Parfit is identical with Wiggins is not so very thrilling, ontologically speaking, if not even Parfit (at one point of time) is identical with Parfit (at another point of time). But it is quite another thing to say that the boundary between individuals therefore is less deep or definite. That two nations merely consist of territories and citizens, and that the citizens at least successively replace each others, does not imply that the boundary between the two nations is not fixed. Would it be more definite if nations consisted of the *same* individual citizens all the time? The abyss between different consciousnesses is as deep irrespective of how you describe the relation between successive states of consciousness, ascribed to the same individual. If we borrow Parfit's analogy between persons and nations we see furthermore that the difference between two persons is deeper than between two nations, since there are no tourists and immigrants in the soul. I cannot think your thoughts and you cannot have mine (although we might often think similarly).

I believe that this is what we ought to mean if we say that the difference between persons is a "deep" ontological fact. We *can* imagine the world different, so that consciousnesses were not separate in this way. Perhaps we can even develop techniques to cross the border to the consciousness of another person – but in the normal case it is impenetrable, and it is not easier to cross it, even if we have not the same self through life.

What would follow if Parfit's idea of personal identity were correct is that the idea of compensation within a life can be problematic: it is not certain that a great happiness towards the end of life can compensate for severe suffering during childhood as is implicit in the novels of Dickens. But the problem of trading the loss of one person against the gain of another is left untouched.

A hard-boiled utilitarian can of course keep to the idea that the gain of Peterson can compensate for the suffering of Jonson. Let's imagine for instance that Jonson has toothache, while Peterson has not (he is not suffering at all). We have only one dose of morphine, which we can give to either of them. Let us further assume that the morphine given to Jonson would make his toothache wither away, but have no other effects. Given to Peterson it would make him hilarious, in fact he would be so happy, that he would gladly accept a toothache as intense as Jonson's for the same time at some other time in order to get this experience. So would Jonson. The utilitarian would have to say that we ought to give Peterson the morphine (if we must give it it to one of them now). But this seems unacceptable, just because they are two different consciousnesses, and we don't find it acceptable to sacrifice Jonson for the happiness of a different individual. And Parfit's Humean (and Buddhist) conception of the self will not give the utilitarian any further support. Only if a Hinduist theory could be made plausible – all experiences are as a matter of fact parts of the same gigantic consciousness – would we get an argument to the effect that we can ignore the differences between persons. But as the world is, the fact that there are distinct individuals with interests is the point of departure for ethics. If there were no more individuals than myself, I would have no moral obligations. I believe – contrary to Parfit – that I would not even have an obligation to populate the world with happy generations for the future, if I had this option in my power. This leads directly to another of Parfit's arguments against rights-based moral theories: that they cannot solve questions concerning what to do in relation to future generations.

2. A moral principle formulated in terms of rights is person-affecting in a way that Derek Parfit tries to show is irrational. Parfit has formulated several arguments to the effect that moral principles cannot be person-affecting in a strong sense and yet be morally acceptable in all situations. If his arguments are sound, we have strong reasons not to accept any moral theory formulated in terms of rights – at least if such a theory is taken to be ultimate and to cover all important moral questions concerning the interests of others.

Parfit's arguments are all tied to moral problems concerning as yet non-existent persons. He argues that moral theories of rights do not answer all moral questions about what to do "to" future generations. I have put "to" in quotation marks since the duties referred to are not strictly duties towards anyone – they are duties by virtue of certain consequences involving the existence or non-existence of these people. But it is very hard to express this without using some such formulation which shows how permeated our moral language is with the idea that good and evil is something which we do to others. The question now is whether this idea is a mistake or are there sound reasons in favour of it. Parfit tries to show that there are good arguments against.

I will argue that what's wrong with Parfit's argument is that he does not distinguish between the two questions: 1. "Which state is better (worse)?" and 2. "Which state ought we to bring about (prevent)?" For the sake of argument I will not disagree with Parfit insofar as questions about value are concerned. But the important question in ethics is "What ought we to do?" And this question is not automatically answered, when we know which actions will have the best consequences.

As was hinted earlier, I find T.M. Scanlon's proposed way of justifying actions attractive (Scanlon 1982). If Scanlon is right, no one can act wrongly unless there is someone who can reasonably complain of the action. I cannot see that such a theory would yield unacceptable results. Let's take those people affected by the risky policy (Parfit 1984, 371 ff): if we choose an energy policy involving the burial of nuclear waste, we make our society different in so many other aspects that the people living 300 years from now are completely different from those that would have lived, if we had chosen a different and less risky policy. Now these people living in the future will have satisfying lives for 40 years and then die from some catastrophe which releases radiation. As

Parfit has constructed the example, these individuals have no reason to complain – if Parfit had not buried the nuclear waste which kills them at the age of forty, they would not have existed. The people who would have been born, had Parfit not buried the waste, cannot complain – they do not exist, *if* he buried the waste. So what are we to say: the outcome where happy people live longer is better than the outcome where happy people are killed before growing old. This is one reason in favour of choosing the less risky policy. Since we can never predict the consequences of our actions in such a remote future with any certainty, we cannot be interested in the problem of how we ought to deliberate and choose. Our only concern can be with the rightness or wrongness of the action. Torbjörn Tännsjö (1978) has proposed that moral properties can apply only to performed actions. If Parfit performed the risky policy, there is no one to complain, he therefore acted rightly. (This is not a conclusion Tännsjö would accept, since he is a hard-boiled utilitarian.) *Had* he instead chosen the less risky alternative, he would of course also have acted rightly, as no one would complain in that case either.

In this way we get somewhat imprecise answers; but this is quite in accordance with our intuitions. We look for effects upon persons (and other living beings), when we consider whether an action was right or wrong. The theory of morals as some kind of convention explains our lack of unambiguous intuitions in cases like Parfit's and this lack of certainty in turn confirms our theory of ethics.

Scanlon's proposal furthermore explains the asymmetry we feel there is between begetting a suffering child and not begetting a happy child – in the former case there is someone who can reasonably complain. In the latter case there is no one. Had we begotten the happy child, no one would have complained either, so we would have acted rightly. It does not seem odd to me that the rightness or wrongness of actions partly depends upon whether or not they are performed. This is especially the case when possible people are concerned. Merely possible people – those who never come into existence – do not pose any moral (or other) claims. Thus this does not mean that we can make the whole earth explode and terminate mankind, since there *are* people who would complain against being killed. But stopping to propagate is not wrong, since if we do, no one will be in the position to complain.

A somewhat harder case is presented by Parfit (1984, 406): let us suppose that we have to choose between two hells. In one ten persons suffer severe agony for 50 years, their agony is so great that they would prefer to die, but they cannot, for some reason or other. The second hell is similar to the first, but there ten million persons suffer the same agony for 49 years and 364 days. Thus a rational person ought for himself to choose the second one. But this is the wrong answer to the question "Which hell ought we to bring about, if we must choose one of them?" according to Parfit. Therefore the question "Which society would a rational person prefer to live in?" is the wrong question to ask: contractualism will yield the wrong answers.

But if instead we use the method proposed by Scanlon we get an acceptable answer, although his idea too fits into the contractualist tradition. In the case of the two hells it seems that in both versions people would have something to complain about, namely that they are not allowed to die. It seems very difficult indeed to make the example realistic in a way that would explain why this would be impossible. But if we accept the assumptions and use the method of Scanlon, we get the answer wanted by Parfit: even if the ten persons in the first hell have slightly more to complain about – one more day of suffering – in the second hell there are so immensely more persons to complain, that we clearly ought to prefer hell one.

Since there are no sound objections against person-affecting moral principles and our intuitions, the over-all explanation of these intuitions by T.M. Scanlon and reasonable theories about the nature of ethics tell strongly in favour of such principles, I conclude that we can accept such principles.

3. A utilitarian might be willing to go a long way in my company as I emphasize the satisfaction of needs. He could argue that the rise in utility brought about by satisfaction of needs is so dramatic that as a matter of fact when choosing between satisfaction of needs for some and desires for others, a utilitarian calculus will almost always favour the choice of the first action. The exception would be situations where you could very significantly render many lives better by sacrificing a few. In such situations the utilitarian could challenge the view expressed by the principle I propose, by asking what use it is to save people to lead lives which are barely worth living. There are situations – most clearly manifested in health care – where the satisfaction of the needs of one individual demands so much of the resources available that there is not much left for caring about satisfaction of desires for other individuals. It seems unreasonable to use all the resources just to save one individual, if you are thereby forced to lower the quality of life so much for many others that their lives contain very few moments of joy and pleasure above a basic level of need-satisfaction. David Braybrooke (1987) is of the opinion that in such situations the claims of needs simply loose their force. We cannot go so far in emphasizing the importance of

needs, according to Braybrooke.

I have in another context (Ohlsson 1979) argued that it is not unreasonable that a great many people refrain from a lot of desire-satisfaction in order to save the life of one individual. But there is probably a limit, where it is no longer morally defensible to lower the standard of well-being of many people to save just one individual. What is the point of living if we are never allowed to do anything but save each other to lead lives that are barely bearable? The point of guaranteeing everyone an acceptable life seems to disappear if the minimally acceptable life becomes the peak of attainment for everyone. So far we must acknowledge the point of the utilitarian.

What seems unacceptable in the utilitarian theory is the possibility that the mere addition of very small increases of utility for different individuals who each have a life well worth living, would in the end amount to a sum of intrinsic value which could outweigh the severe suffering or death of some other individual(s) (cf Ohlsson 1979). I think we have to take some middle path. If we use the method proposed by T.M. Scanlon referred to earlier, that ethics requires that we can justify our actions to those concerned, I believe that we can reach an acceptable solution.

Charles Fried (1970) has pointed out that we are all prepared to take some risks in order to live good lives. Who would dare to fall in love, drink wine or even take a walk, if she always put survival and avoidance of suffering in the first place? We must risk not only our own lives, but also take some risks with the lives of others in order to be able to live a normal life. Of course we are not allowed to take greater risks with the lives of others, not even equal risks, but there are some risks we must take. Fried therefore proposes that we accept an idea about a "risk-pool" from which we draw our just share: we are allowed to take some normal risks with others and if for some reason we have taken more than our share, we must be more than usually careful for some time. When we have some very important goal (important not only to ourselves, but in general social terms) we are allowed to take greater risks than usual. But the general rule is that "we may not deliberately confront others with a grave risk of death so long as we have any choice in the matter" (Fried 1970, 200).

In so called welfare societies health care institutions are organized and financed in a way which could be considered as a kind of collective insurance against the worst outcomes, if someone is unfortunate to get a serious disease or is afflicted by some accident, we all collectively contribute to his recovery. We are all guaranteed the same treatment should the misfortune afflict us. But at the same time we collectively decide how much resources we are prepared to abstain from in order to get this guarantee. Now I am not arguing that the actual level of health care and the resources we put into health care are the morally defensible ones. I believe that most people in the hope of remaining healthy are too restrictive and shortsightedly want to keep their money for consumption. Furthermore both money and the risks of getting ill and handicapped are unequally distributed, so that those who have least money also are those who have the greatest risks of becoming ill and handicapped in their work. Therefore the resources put aside for health care are likely to be insufficient. But if the risks and the pecuniary resources were equally distributed I believe that some agreement could be reached about which level of health care would be a reasonable compromise between the desire to be able to satisfy desires above the mere level of need-satisfaction and the primary interest of a minimally acceptable survival. No one can be certain that she will not belong to the unfortunate group and would therefore be prepared to take some measures to guarantee that if she was struck by misfortune there would be enough resources to save her for a life worth living. On the other hand even the very risk-aversive person would realize that in some situations it would be unreasonable to use immense sums of money to save someone for a slightly longer life, when this would mean that both he and many others would have the level of satisfaction drastically decreased for the rest of their lives.

We are thus forced to admit the strength of this argument and modify the proposed principle accordingly: the satisfaction of needs will be given lexical priority in all cases except when the members of society have unanimously agreed to some form of insurance system which determines the level of acceptable risks for death, suffering and severe handicaps. If they have unanimously agreed to accept some risks in order to increase the general quality of life, then it is not unacceptable if someone is left to die or suffer, if saving his life would be so costly that it would render the lives of the healthy (including the sick person himself before he was struck by his misfortune) just barely acceptable. This might seem very vague; furthermore it seems as if we have given in to the utilitarian. But if we rescue this patient although her illness is not included among those we have decided to rescue individuals from, this one case would not raise the taxes in a remarkable way; so it could be argued that she is sacrificed for very marginal improvements of the lives of others. But to this must be added some idea of equal treatment – if this patient is to be saved, others with the same kind of illness and the same needs for costly treatment should have it too. And that would be too costly. Thus we have to decide some limit where we no longer

do everything possible to save individual lives.
  This might be a point where the utilitarian is right – it *is* unreasonable to let many people's lives be barely acceptable in order to save one individual for a few hours more of a life which is just possible to endure. But what is not acceptable in utilitarianism is the possibility that the suffering or death of someone can be morally justified by it's making other people's lives trivially better, provided that these latter are sufficiently numerous. This is not allowed by my principles: you cannot get anyone to accept that it is reasonable that he is suffering just in order to let others experience a little more pleasure (provided they are fairly happy at the outset). So this is a demarcation line. It is possible that the utilitarian can make even this difference disappear: by counting trivial pleasures as carrying very little value, or by not accepting the addition of small quantities of happiness. If he does the result might be the same. But on the other hand this device seems very much *ad hoc*, and designed to avoid the criticism. If the result is that the same actions will be permitted and the same forbidden, I have nothing to object as then the utilitarian will have adjusted his theory to meet my objection. On the other hand I have modified my theory in the light of his objection. But it is also possible to justify this modification internally and if we use the method proposed by Scanlon, we can argue that it would be very difficult to get everyone to accept that it is reasonable that they all forsake almost every desire-satisfaction in order to save someone for a little longer just bearable life.

4. The utilitarian has still another objection to a theory of rights in asking if there is any point in guaranteeing the rights of people, if they don't use them to make their lives better? In other words, is not the important thing that people are satisfied – not that the necessary means to satisfaction are safeguarded? What is the use of these necessary means if people nevertheless don't become satisfied? Therefore, the utilitarian argues, it is better – when it comes to formulating a criterion of rightness, not rules of thumb – to go straight for the goal: satisfaction. First of all I want to stress that what someone *needs* according to my analysis, is to *do* something with the thing needed. You do not just need food – you need to eat food. Thus you cannot object that according to my theory people have a right to food, but suppose they do not eat the food, would it not have been better to give it to others? The right to need-satisfaction is a right to get the needs satisfied, i.e. to have, use, consume the object which only elliptically is said to be needed. Your right to food is not satisfied by just giving you food if you do not eat it (except in those cases where you voluntarily starve in order to reach

some goal of yours, of course). Let us consider some cases where resources might seem to get wasted if you keep to my theory:
A. Peterson gets his needs satisfied, but is killed in a car accident.
B. Peterson gets his needs satisfied, but takes his life.
C. Peterson gets his needs satisfied, but gets no desires satisfied.

Let us assume that in all three cases the resources used for satisfaction of the needs of Peterson could instead have been used for the satisfaction of the desires of others (but not for satisfying the needs of others).

In situation A you cannot say that the resources are wasted: if you had used them for other goals, this would have meant that Peterson had suffered before he was killed, or that he would have died earlier in order to render more desires for other people satisfied. This is not morally acceptable. The same can be said about situation B. But in that case you might even question the truth of what is said. If Peterson suffers from some endocrine depression, anxiety or some such illness, then his basic needs are not satisfied after all. If his suicide is not caused by any such mental disturbance it must be motivated by some personal project: he does not want to live when his girlfriend has left him or when his country has been occupied. This might be the case, but you cannot reasonably claim that the resources have been spoilt, simply because he commits suicide. Frustrating his needs had meant that he either had died earlier or that his life up to his death had not been worth living. It is not acceptable to make Peterson suffer or kill him earlier, just because we happen to know that he will kill himself in a few days. To a utilitarian it cannot be important that a person lives a "full" life or else his life would be valueless. That could be the standpoint of someone who took personal development, maturity or something such like to have intrinsic value, but it could hardly be the standpoint of a utilitarian. Neither is it my position, although I find it important that every individual is at least able to have a life worth living.

The case of C is not much more difficult. Either his life is so miserable because of continuous desire frustration that it is not worth living. Then it is not strictly true that all his needs have been satisfied – *some* desires must be satisfied if your life is not to be felt totally meaningless, thus some satisfaction of desire is *necessary*, some satisfaction of desire is a need. Or else his life is worth living after all, in which case it would be wrong to take his life to render the lives of others who are not bad off, still better.

But a fourth case is possible: D. We can satisfy some but not all of Peterson's needs. Are we still to try to satisfy those needs that we can rather than use the resources for other aims? First of all it should be noticed that I have defined needs as necessary and in the situation sufficient means to reach an acceptable life. This means that if, for instance, the person has neither food nor water, and another person has water but no food, and we can deliver food but no water to just one of them, we ought to give it to the second. The first one does not even need food strictly speaking: he needs food *and* water.

But there is a substantial moral question involved in some such situations it seems to me, and a question without a given answer. Hitherto I have presumed that satisfaction of needs is all or nothing: either all your needs are satisfied or you die or your life is not worth living. But death can be postponed for a few hours and there are different levels even in hell. Is it then more important to postpone death for a few minutes than to satisfy a lot of desires? Is it better to decrease suffering, however little it may be, rather than make a lot of people more satisfied? As a general rule I believe that we would usually answer these questions in the affirmative, and that this would be the correct answer. But I have respect for those who answer them in the negative. Especially when the postponement is very short and the mitigation of the suffering is hardly noticeable, it seems that the urgency of suffering and death withers away. If and only if Peterson has some prospects of a meaningful life, is there a point in satisfying those of his needs that are connected with survival. This is the reason why I have defined "basic needs" as "necessary and in the situation sufficient" conditions for an acceptable life. But this life needs not be very long: even a few moments of a life can be meaningful. (Perhaps it is just a few moments of each life that are really worth living?) It is very difficult to give any directions on how long the remaining life should be to count, or how many desires must be satisfied to render life worth living. This must be left for individual decisions.

Even if it seems as if I have conceded to the utilitarian at this point too, I don't think that I have conceded too much: the utilitarian is prepared to frustrate the needs of someone even if she were to get a satisfactory life for years, if he could thereby increase the desire-satisfaction for a lot of individuals just very little, provided that the group satisfied was large enough. This is not allowed by the theory considered here.

5. Now we come to the most difficult of the objections against the proposed theory: who are included among the right-holders and on what grounds? The idea behind contractualist reasoning in ethics has usually been that equals agree to respect each others rights. If you respect my rights, I will respect yours. This idea both has its attractive and its appalling features. I have already touched upon the attractive ones – now

I will point to the converse. To be a right-holder you must qualify by being a person with whom we can make an agreement.You must be at least minimally rational, and you must not be too weak – if you are weak I need not reciprocally sign a contract with you, I could just exploit you. Most theories of rights have ascribed rights to human beings or some group of human beings. These rights have been grounded in some property which has been assumed to be characteristic of human beings in general or of the members of the privileged group. A theory of rights therefore has a fragrance of an exclusive club: "Membership of our club is open to everyone who fulfills condition V, and who furthermore sticks to the rules of the club." [5]

The idea that you have to go through a test to qualify to be treated morally seems repugnant. Seen from this perspective, theories of rights seem to specify the privileges of some group in relation to other groups. The original declarations of rights – *Magna Charta* for example – explicitly state which group is to be ascribed rights. And in the English Revolution in the 17th century many of the revolutionaries thought that only property-owners were to have the right to vote. Even a declaration of human rights declares the rights to belong to human beings as against the animals e.g. Moreover most actual contracts are as a matter of fact unfair because they are bargained from very unequal positions of strength. Could "moral contracts" be very different? It seems as if many weak and handicapped persons would never enter the contract: the strong ones are not dependent upon them. The animals would be left out too, since they cannot come to a reciprocal agreement at all, at least not in written form. David Gauthier's theory (1986) is an example of a contract theory with these implications.

But we seem to have moral obligations towards the weak and also towards animals (not to treat them cruelly for instance). Indeed, our duties towards the weak seem especially strong morally speaking.

Therefore it seems as if a theory of rights cannot be the basis of a moral theory, at any rate our duties towards animals cannot be inferred from rights, at least not if the rights are taken to be grounded on a reciprocal convention.

On the other hand there have been attempts to ascribe animals rights; Tom Regan, *The Case for Animal Rights*, 1983, is the best example

---

[5] As a matter of fact there is at least one philosopher who has proposed that you look upon human rights as a kind of rules of a game, which we voluntarily take upon us to make life a little more difficult and thereby more exciting to live: K.R. Minogue, 1978!

hitherto.

I want to stress once more that in my theory the moral force of need-claims does not emanate from an agreement – whether actual or hypothetical. The moral force of need-claims – and consequently of the right-claims – comes from the urgency of needs and from the interests we have. We all want to live acceptable lives and satisfy our desires. We therefore want rules established which guarantee our possibility of getting our needs satisfied and our possibility to strive for satisfaction of our desires. Therefore it is reasonable to include among the individuals covered by the rules all individuals who have interests.

On the other hand we have a subjective reason to respect these rules only in relation to those whom we depend upon. Therefore the moral system at first includes only human beings in our close vicinity, whom we need in order to get our vital interests satisfied. When we come to realize, however, the mutual interdependence of human beings in general, and furthermore the mutual interdependence of all living organisms, we can widen the moral realm. We then realize that other beings have interests similar to our own. Their claims are as justified as our own. Of course my own subjective reason to help other beings satisfy their needs and to abstain from interfering with their desire-satisfaction will be diminished in proportion to their capacity to influence my satisfaction of interests. This however does not diminish the force of their claims – only my subjective disposition to acknowledge their claims. Thus animals and weak human beings are included in the moral realm, although their interests and claims can come into conflict with my own. But since I want a system of rules institutionalized to safeguard my vital interests, I can realize that the same is true of all beings with interests. I therefore can see, at least abstractly, that the system of rights should not be limited to cover just those close to me, although I am most inclined to respect the rights of those whom I have the most to gain from. But this seems to fit our moral praxis: we tend to respect the rights of those close to us to a higher degree than those very far away. This does not mean that we deny that these others also have rights and legitimate claims.

You might object that I am mixing up the question about the origin of morals and the question about the validation of moral requirements. In a way I am – I want to view morality as a natural phenomenon and at the same time find a method for validating moral claims. I have tried to make it plausible that the method proposed by T.M. Scanlon can have both functions. But I am not quite sure that it works. First of all, what does it mean to say that animals have *rights*? We cannot reasonably say that they can raise right-claims – they cannot, as far as we know, have an idea of an institutionalized system of rules. But is this necessary?

It would be unreasonable to deny that higher animals have interests. If they could, they would claim rights just as we do. But of course it is up to us to recognize their rights. It is true that I have made no attempts to spell out the rights of animals. But I do believe that it is possible to widen the realm of right-holders to include animals.

However it is doubtful if it can be done along the lines I have sketched for human rights. But it seems to me as if our moral consciousness gradually became more inclusive: in the beginning we just considered the claims of our family and relatives. The circle widened to include human beings of our own town or country. Nowadays few deny the rights of all human beings (except in practice). Some have also included the animals; forerunners have been the Hindus, the Buddhists, and in the Christian world S:t Francis. The cause for animal rights is argued by many moral philosophers in our days.

Seen in this light moral claims are not inexplicably queer, being both natural and normative (cf Mackie, 1977). Moral claims are claims put forward by others which you sometimes subscribe to just to safeguard your own interests. A model of this kind of reasoning is provided by David Gauthier's *Morals by Agreement* (1986). But his view is not mine: I am arguing that we claim a right to need-satisfaction just because this is our prime interest. The moral force does not emanate from the contract. What Gauthier tries to show is that in many cases we also have a subjective (egotistical) reason for complying with these requirements. I have no quarrel with that standpoint. But I want to insist that the urgency of moral claims comes exclusively from the necessity of satisfying needs.

It might not be true that we are exclusively or mainly egotists, so that we must always be motivated by self-interest in a narrow sense. Many of us seem capable of recognizing the claims of others and also of foregoing some satisfaction of self-related desires to satisfy the needs and desires of others. Perhaps Hume was not so wrong after all in maintaining that we all have some fellow-feeling with others. Interest in the well-being of others can also be part of our motivation, as Butler pointed out.[6]

It seems as if a narrow conception of 'rationality', taking it to be rational always to try to maximize one's own utility, can be self-

---

[6] Joseph Butler, *Sermons*, Sermon I §4, Sermon XI, and elsewhere. Several editions, see for instance the edition by W.E. Gladstone, Oxford 1897.

defeating in many situations, especially situations like the prisoner's dilemma. In such situations our rational self-interest can exhort us to make choices which do not have as good consequences as would have choices according to principles of cooperation. In such situations a shift from egotistical rationality to my principles of respect for rights for instance, gives better results. We all benefit in the long run from living in a society where rights are respected. Therefore we have a reason to try to uphold such moral principles. And although we can be tempted to violate the rights of others in some situations, we ought not. We do not always have an egotistical rational reason to respect them. But the principle condemns such behaviour, i.e. such behaviour is quite simply wrong.

When it comes to the problem of finding reasonable solutions to conflicts of interests we have to reason in several steps. The first step is that it is plausible to accept reciprocal obligations to respect the rights of some other equals. This is clearly rationally justified for most of us. The second step is the acknowledgement that I could get into a situation where I need the help of others but cannot help them. To get some insurance against being left without help in such a situation, I have an interest in institutionalizing moral norms which make it obligatory to help those in need. You can easily imagine yourself placed in a situation of severe misery and in need of help. In short you can identify yourself with the needy.

The last step is a kind of analogous reasoning when it comes to very small children, handicapped persons, and animals. We can at least in some way imagine what it would be like for an animal to be treated cruelly. After all we are all animals and the basic needs are common to all higher mammals at least. We also begin to be aware that we are more caught in a complicated and tightly woven web of ecological interdependence than we used to believe. We therefore also have some egotistical reasons to respect other forms of living organisms. However, these are of course weaker than the reasons for coming to an agreement with some of our nearest companions.This explains the difficulty in getting the rights of animals recognized. But identification and analogous reasoning shows that there are at least some claims on behalf of animals that are morally urgent.

I have not argued that moral claims emanate from a social contract. I have argued that they emanate from urgent claims that we – human beings and animals alike – have because of our needs.

Bibliography

Anscombe, Elisabeth, "Modern Moral Philosophy", *Philosophy*, Vol XXXIII No 124 (1958): 1-19.
Aristotle, *Nichomachean Ethics*.
Barry, Brian, *Political Argument*, London: Routledge & Kegan Paul, 1965.
—— *The Liberal Theory of Justice*, London: Oxford University Press, 1973.
Benn, Stanley Isaac & Peters, Richard S., *Social Principles and the Democratic State*, London: Allen & Unwin, 1959.
Bentham, Jeremy, *An Introduction to the Principles of Morals and Legislation*, Oxford 1789; quotations from the 1879 edition.
Bergström, Lars, "What is a Conflict of Interest?" *Journal of Peace Research*, No 3 (1970): 197-217.
Blanc, Louis, *Organisation du Travail*, 1st ed, Paris, 1839; quotations from 9th ed, Paris: Bureau du Nouveau Monde, 1850.
Brandt, Richard B., *A Theory of the Good and the Right*, Oxford: Clarendon Press, 1979.
"The Concept of a Moral Right and Its Function." *The Journal of Philosophy*, Vol. LXXX, No1 (1983): 29-45.
Braybrooke, David, "Let Needs Diminish that Preferences May Prosper." *Studies in Moral Philosophy,* ed. by Nicholas Rescher, Oxford: Blackwell, 1968.
—— *Meeting Needs*, Princeton, N.J.: Princeton University Press, 1987.
Butler, Joseph, *Sermons*, ed. W.E. Gladstone, Oxford, 1897
Carlyle, R.W. & Carlyle, A.J., *A History of Mediæval Political Theory in the West*, Vol II, Edinburgh and London, William Blackwell and Sons, 1909.
Castoriadis, Cornelius, *Les carrefours du labyrinthe*, Collections Esprits, 1978. (Transl.: *Crossroads in the Labyrinth*, Cambridge, Mass.: MIT Press, 1984.)

Cicero, *De finibus.*
Cofer, C. N. & Appley, M. H., *Motivation: Theory and Research*, New York: John Wiley & Sons, 1964.
Duncker, Karl, "On Pleasure, Emotion, and Striving", *Philosophy and Phenomenological Research*, Vol I, (1940): 391-430.
Egonson, Dan, *Interests, Utilitarianism and Moral Standing*, Lund: Lund University Press, 1990.
Fitzgerald, Ross, "Abraham Maslow's Hierarchy of Needs – An Exposition and Evaluation." *Human Needs and Politics*, ed. Fitzgerald, Rushcutters Bay: Pergamon Press, 1977.
Flew, Antony, "Wants or Needs, Choices or Commands", *Human Needs and Politics*, ed. by Ross Fitzgerald, Rushcutters Bay: Pergamon Press, 1977.
Frankena, William, *Ethics*, Englewood Cliffs, N.J.: Prentice-Hall, 1963.
—— "Some Beliefs about Justice", The Lindley Lecture, University of Kansas 1966.
Fried, Charles, *An Anatomy of Values*, Cambridge, Mass.: Harvard University Press, 1970.
Gauthier, David, *Morals by Agreement*, Oxford: Clarendon Press, 1986.
Griffin, James, *Well-being*, Oxford: Clarendon Press, 1986.
Hare, Richard M., *Freedom and Reason*, Oxford: Oxford University Press, 1963.
—— *Moral Thinking*, Oxford: Clarendon Press, 1981.
Harsanyi, John C, "Morality and the theory of rational behaviour", *Utilitarianism and Beyond*, ed. A. Sen and B. Williams, Cambridge: Cambridge University Press, 1982.
Hegel, Friedrich, *Grundlinien des Philosophie des Rechts*, 1821.
Heller, Agnes, *Bedeutung und Funktion des Begriffs Bedürfnis im Denken von Karl Marx*, 1974, translated as *The Theory of Need in Marx*, , New York: St Martin's Press, 1976.
Heller, Joseph, *Catch 22*, New York: Simon & Schuster, 1961.
Hobbes, Thomas, *Leviathan*, 1651.
Horney, Karen, "Das neurotische Liebesbedürfnis", *Zentralblatt für Psychotherapie* 10 (1937).
Hull, Clark L., *The Principles of Behaviour*, New York: Appleton-Century-Crofts, Inc.,1943.
Hume, David, *An Enquiry Concerning the Principles of Morals.* 1751 second edition 1777.
Illitch, Ivan, *Towards a History of Needs*, New York: Pantheon, 1977.
Jaeger,Werner, *Paideia* I, Berlin, 1934; 4th edition Berlin: Walter de

Gruyter & Co, 1959.
James, William, *The Will to Believe and Other Essays in Popular Philosophy,* New York: Longmans, Green and Company, 1897.
Kant, Immanuel, *Grundlegung zur Metaphysik der Sitten,* Zweyte Auflage, Riga: Johann Friedrich Hartnoch, 1786.
Kenny, Anthony, *Will, Freedom, and Power,* Oxford: Blackwell, 1975.
Leiss, William, *The Limits to Satisfaction: on Needs and Commodities*, Toronto: University of Toronto Press, 1976. New edition London: Boyars, 1978.
Lewis, Clarence Irving, *An Analysis of Knowledge and Valuation*, La Salle, Illinois: Open Court, 1946.
—— *The Ground and Nature of the Right*, New York: Columbia University Press, 1955.
Lovejoy, A.O.& Boas, B., *Primitivism and Related Ideas in Antiquity*, John Hopkins, 1935; quotations from the 1965 edition, New York: Octagon Books.
Lucretius, *De rerum natura.*
McCloskey, H.J., "Human needs, Rights and Political Values", *American Philosophical Quarterly*, Vol 13, No1 (Jan. 1976): 1-11.
McHale, John & McHale, Magda Cordell, *Basic Human Needs*, New Brunswick, N.J.: Transaction Books, 1978.
Mackie, John L, *Ethics - Inventing Right and Wrong,* Harmondsworth: Penguin, 1977.
Marcuse, Herbert, *One-dimensional Man*, Boston: Beacon, 1964.
Marx, Karl, *Die deutsche Ideologie*, 1845-46
—— *Das Kapital*, 1867
—— *Kritik des Gothaer Programms*, 1875
—— *Kritik der Politischen Ökonomie,* 1903
All quotations from Marx & Engels, *Werke*, Berlin: Dietz Verlag, 1972
Maslow, Abraham, "A Theory of Human Motivation", *Psychological Review*, Vol 50 (1943).
—— *Motivation and Personality*, New York: Harper & Row, Publishers, 1954 (new edition 1970).
—— *The Farther Reaches of Human Nature*, New York: Viking, 1971.
Mill, John Stuart, *Utilitarianism*, London, 1863; quotations from the Everyman's Library edition, London 1964.
Miller, David, *Social Justice*, Oxford: Clarendon Press, 1976.
Minogue, K.R., "Natural Rights, Ideology and the Game of Life", *Human Rights,* ed. Kamenka, E. & Tay, A.E, London: Edward Arnold, 1978.
Moore, George Edward, *Principia Ethica*, Cambridge: Cambridge University Press, 1903.

Morgan, Clifford T., "Physiological Theory of Drive", *Introduction to Psychology*, New York: McGraw-Hill Book Company, 1956.
Morris, William, *News from Nowhere*, 1888.; references to *Three Works by William Morris*, London: Lawrence & Wishart, 1977.
Murray, H.A., et al, *Explorations in Personality*, New York: Oxford University Press, 1938.
Nielsen, Kai, "On Human Needs and Moral Appraisals", *Inquiry*, vol 6 (1963): 170-183.
—"Morality and Needs", *The Business of Reason*, ed. by MacIntosh, J. J. & Coval S., London: Routledge & Kegan Paul, 1969.
Nozick, Robert, *Anarchy, State, and Utopia*, Oxford: Basil Blackwell, 1974.
Ohlsson, Ragnar, *The Moral Import of Evil. On counterbalancing death, suffering, and degradation*. Stockholm: Akademilitteratur, 1979.
Parfit, Derek, *Reasons and Persons*, Oxford: Clarendon Press, 1984.
Perry, Ralph Barton, *General Theory of Value. Its Meaning and Basic Principles in Terms of Interest*,Cambridge, Mass.: Harvard University Press, 1926, reissued 1950.
Peters, Richard S., *The Concept of Motivation*, London: Routledge & Kegan Paul, 1958.
Plant, Raymond, Lesser, Harry & Taylor-Gooby, Peter, *Political Philosophy and Social Welfare. Essays on the Normative Basis of Welfare Provision*, London: Routledge and Kegan Paul, 1980.
Plato, *The Republic*.
— *Gorgias*.
Pontara, Giuliano, "Utilitarism, lycka och jämlikhet" ("Utilitarianism, happiness, and equality"), *Filosofisk tidskrift*, No 3, (1985): 1-13.
Popper, Karl Raimund, *The Open Society and Its Enemies*, London: Routledge & Kegan Paul, 1945.
Rawls, John, *A Theory of Justice*, Oxford:Oxford University Press, 1972.
Regan, Tom, *The Case for Animal Rights*, Berkeley: University of California Press, 1983.
Rescher, Nicholas, *Distributive Justice*, Indianapolis & New York: Bobbs-Merril, 1966.
Sartre, Jean Paul, *L'etre et le néant*, Paris: Gallimard, 1943.
— *Critique de la raison dialectique*, Paris: Gallimard, 1960.
Scanlon, T.M., "Contractualism and Utilitarianism", *Utilitarianism and Beyond*, ed. Sen, A. & Williams, B., Cambridge: Cambridge University Press, 1982.
Seneca, *The 90th letter to Lucilius*.

Sekora, John, *Luxury. The Concept in Western Thought*, Baltimore: John Hopkins University Press, 1977.
Sidgwick, Henry, *The Methods of Ethics*, 7th ed. London: Macmillan, 1907; quotations from the 1966 printing.
Soper, Kate, *On Human Needs. Open and Closed Theories in a Marxist Perspective*. Sussex: The Harvester Press, 1981.
Springborg, Patricia, *The Problem of Human Needs and the Critique of Civilization*, London: Allen & Unwin, 1981.
Sterba, James P., *The Demands of Justice*, Notre Dame: University of Notre Dame Press, 1980.
Streeten, Paul, et al., *First Things First*, World Bank, 1981.
Sørlander, Kai, "Om behov" ("On needs"), *Filosofisk tidskrift*, no 2 (1989): 20-32.
Taylor, Paul, "'Need' Statements", *Analysis*, Vol 19, No 5 (1959): 106-111.
Thomson, Garrett, *Needs*, London: Routledge & Kegan Paul, 1987.
Tierney, B, *Medieval Poor Law*, Berkeley: University of California Press, 1959.
Tranøy, Knut Erik, *On the Logic of Normative Systems*, 1953 "Asymmetries in Ethics", *Inquiry*, Vol 10 (1967): 351-372.
"'Ought' Implies 'Can': A Bridge from Fact to Norm", *Ratio*, Vol XIV (1972): 116-130 & XVII (1975): 147-175.
Tännsjö, Torbjörn, "The Morality of Abstract Entities", *Theoria*, Vol XLIV (1978): 1-18.
—"Against Berlin", *Archiv für Rechts- und Sozialphilosophie,* Vol 71 (1985): 218-233
— *Moral Realism*, Totowa, N.J.: Rowman & Littlefield, 1990 (1990 I).
— *Vårdetik (Ethics of Caring)*, Stockholm: Rabén & Sjögren, 1990 (1990 II).
Walsh, V.C., *Scarcity and Evil*, Englewood Cliffs, N.J.: Spectrum Books, 1961.
Wawrzinek, Utta Kim, "Bedürfnis", *Geschichtliche Grundbegriffe*, ed. Brunner, Conze, & Koselleck, Stuttgart: Ernst Klett Verlag, 1972.
Weil, Simone, *L'enracimement*, Paris: Gallimard, 1949, quotation from 28th ed., Paris 1952.
White, Alan R., *Modal Thinking*, Oxford: Blackwell, 1975.
Wiggins, David, "Claims of Need", *Morality and Objectivity*, to J.L. Mackie, ed. Honderich, Ted, London: Routledge & Kegan Paul, 1985; also in Wiggins, *Needs, Values, Truth*, Oxford: Blackwell, 1987.
Winstanley, Gerrard, *Law of Freedom*, 1652. Can be found for instance in *The Works of Gerrard Winstanley*, ed. Sabine, Cornell University

Press, 1941; quotations from the second edition New York: Russell & Russell, 1965.

von Wright, Georg Henrik, *Explanation and Understanding*, Ithaca, N.Y.: Cornell University Press, 1971.

—— *Norm and Action,* London: Routledge & Kegan Paul, 1963 (1963 I).

—— *The Varieties of Goodness,* London: Routledge & Kegan Paul, 1963 (1963 II).

——"Om behov" ("On Needs"), *Filosofisk tidskrift,* No 1 (1982): 1-12.

Young, P.T., "Physiological Drives", *International Encyclopaedia of the Social Sciences*, ed. Sills, New York: MacMillan, 1968.

Österberg, Jan, *Self and Others*, Dordrecht: Kluwer Academic Publishers, 1986.

Index

Anscombe, E., 45
Appley, M.H., 40n
Aristotle, 10, 18, 20, 21, 29, 31, 32, 46, 55
autonomy, 8, 17, 67, 85, 111-112

Babeuf F.N., 23
Barry, B., 54, 62
Benn, S., 103n
Bentham, J., 32, 76
Bergström, L. ix, 1
Boas, B., 28-30
Blanc, L. 23
Brandt, R.B., 64, 70, 76, 78, 79, 82n, 85
Braybrooke, D., 44-46, 93, 97, 132, 133
Butler, J. 140

Cabet E., 23
Carlyle, A.J., 21
Carlyle, R.N., 21
Castoriadis, C., 25-26
Cicero, 20
Cofer, C.N. 40n

desire,
 defined as behaviour disposition, 70
 informed, 78-81
 intrinsic, 74-75
 morally suspect, 90-92
 second-order, 73, 81, 83
 self-related, 76-77
 unchangeable, 83
desire-satisfaction, explained, 2
Dickens, C., 91, 129
Duncker, K., 86n

Egonson, D., 71n, 72, 73, 78, 87
Epicurus, 20
ethical egoism, 4n

Fitzgerald, R., 40n
Flew, A., 51, 97
Fourier C., 23
Frankena, W., 56-58
Fried, C., 133

Gauthier, D., 14, 138, 140
Griffin, J., 86-87

Hare, R.M., 78
Harsanyi, J.C., 78
hedonism, 2-3
Hegel, F., 22-24, 27
Heller, A., 24, 26
Heller, J., 108
Hobbes, T., 14
Horney, K., 42n
Hull, C.L., 26, 37
human nature, 18, 21, 22, 28, 29, 31, 33, 109, 122
Hume, D., 140

Illitch, I., 28
interests, 1 et passim
Thomson's analysis of i., 48-50
intrinsic value, 69, 75, 86, 91
intuitions, moral, 13, 115, 120, 126, 127

Jæger, W., 29
James, W., 1-2
justice, 54-64

Kant, I., 9, 122
Kenny, A., 10n
Leiss, W., 27
Lesser, H., 52, 66
Lewis, C.I., 75
Locke, J. 104
Lovejoy, A.O., 28-30
Lucretius, 22

Mably G.B., 23
McCloskey, H.J., 45
McHale, J., 27
McHale, M.C., 27
Mackie, J.L., 6, 14, 120
Marcuse, H., 26, 37-39, 82
Marx, K. 23-26, 31, 33, 41, 58, 100n
Maslow, A. 26, 37, 38, 40-42
maximization, 7, 13, 15, 126, 127
methods of moral philosophy, 13
Mill, J.S., 3, 31, 32
Miller, D., 45, 51, 52, 54-59, 64, 97
Minogue, K.R., 138n
Moore, G.E. 6, 75, 87
Morelly
Morgan, C.T. 37n
Morris, W., 58n
Murray, H.A., 26, 37

needs,
defined, 95
basic needs, defined, 97
relativity of n., 22-26, 33, 98-101
true and false n., 25, 26, 37-39
Nielsen, K., 43, 51, 64, 65, 97
Nozick, R., 117, 121, 122
Ohlsson, R., 133
Owen R., 23
Parfit, D., 5, 8n, 86, 127-132
personal project, 11, 12, 15, 105, 108, 109, 112, 118, 125, 136
Peters, R.S., 51, 103n
Plant, R., 52, 66
Plato, 19-21, 29
Pontara, G., 63
Popper, K.R., 8n
practical syllogism, 10

Rawls, J., 54, 61-63
reason,
moral, 12-18
objectice / subjective, 9-11
Regan, T., 117, 138
Rescher, N., 62,
right, defined, 116
Rousseau, J.J., 22, 23, 25, 28

Saint-Simon, H., 23
Sartre, J.-P., 27
Scanlon, T.M., 120-123, 130-133, 135, 139
Seneca, 20, 22
Sekora, J. 22
Sidgwick, H., 5, 78
Singer, P., 78
Socrates, 29, 30, 31
Soper, K., 26
Sophists, 28, 29, 30
Springborg, P., 21, 24, 27
Sterba, J.P., 54, 63

Stoics, 20, 21, 28
Streeten, P., 27
Sørlander, K., ix, 94n

Taylor, P., 93
Taylor-Gooby, P., 52, 66
Thomson, G., 44, 48-51, 65, 93-94, 97
Tierney, B., 21
Tranøy, K.E., 8n, 44, 51-52, 64-66
Tännsjö, T., ix, 3, 89, 111, 131

utilitarianism, 57, 63, 117, 121, 122, 126, 127, 129, 132-137

Walsh, V.C., 48n
Wawrzinek, U.K., 43
Weil, S., 42n
White, A.R. 93, 96, 97
Wiggins, D., 43, 44, 53, 97, 101
Winstanley, G., 21, 23, 58n
von Wright, G.H., 10, 14, 43, 46-48, 50, 52, 65, 78, 97

Young, P.T., 37n
Österberg, J., ix, , 4n, 90n